LONDO:

Coffee

SHOPS

Researched, compiled and edited by
Shaun Beary, Sophie Goodchild, Paul Wright

HotSpot Publications

Copyright © HotSpot Publications 1996

First published in Great Britain in 1996 by
HotSpot publications

1 3 5 7 9 10 8 6 4 2

ISBN 0 9528322 0 8

HotSpot Publications
9 Leamington Road Villas, London W11 1HS
0171 221 4669

Designed by Katrina ffiske

Printed and bound in Great Britain
by C.B.E. 2000 Birmingham

Not being included in this guide implies no lack of merit.
If your favourite coffee shop is not here please let us know
and we may include it in our next edition.

CONTENTS

To
Barry, Ursula, Michael, Paul,
Kate, Brenda, Emma, Nabil and Marie

Cover and illustrations are by the famous
Middle Eastern artist and writer Nabil A. Hamad, who
has lived in Paris and, now a British citizen, runs the
Argile Gallery Café with his wife Marie Saba.
Other drawings by Penny Amstice (page 27)
and Paddy Rossmore (page 30).

Reviews by Shaun Beary, Sophie Goodchild,
John J. Healey, Neil Norman, Sophie Poklewski-Koziell,
Joanna Robertson, Paul Wright.

Our thanks to Alex, Amanda, Charlotte, Denise, Katrina,
Andrew Knight, Anita Leroy, Marie-Laure, Sue Rowe,
Tamar Yoseloff, Bob White.

INTRODUCTION

Here is our choice of London's Good Coffee Shops. From pop-in stand-up shops, to places you can linger in and read or write while you wait for the day to take shape, or meet people in pleasant, relaxed surroundings, London's coffee shops cater to an increasingly wide and discerning section of its resident and visiting population.

London is where the traditional Italian and English coffee shops have been joined by those run by a truly astonishing array of nationalities with amazing benefits for those of us who go to them. There is food too, whether ambrosia or just good croissants and pastries.

These coffee shops all want to do a good job. So if things aren't as you wish, speak to somebody and give them a chance to explain. We wish you good coffee, good food and good times in London's Good Coffee Shops.

The Editors
0171 221 4669

COFFEE
Ethiopia to England

Coffee is reputed to have been discovered by an Ethiopian goat herd, who noticed his goats being more boisterous than usual and traced the cause to the coffee bushes they were munching.

Coffee travelled to Yemen and Arabia with the Ethiopian army, and in the 13th Century it was introduced to the Moslem World through the Holy cities of Islam, by pilgrims returning home from Mecca and Medina. The Turks took to coffee passionately, and by 1600 it was established in the inns and coffee tents of Turkish garrisons all over the Ottoman Empire. Certainly the Turks brought coffee along when they laid siege to Vienna in 1683, where the Poles grabbed their tents and their coffee.

Soon there were coffee shops in Venice and France. Meanwhile coffee had arrived and taken hold in London, where, by the middle of the 17th Century, things were going along nicely for the coffee trade. By 1699 there were five hundred coffee shops, most with their own regulars. There were meeting places for writers, politicians, clergymen, wits, lawyers, Frenchmen, Scots, and so forth. Enterprising owners offered facilities from taking in mail and providing news sheets, to services more 'personal'. Some even minted their own money.

A dream coffee house

A modern dream coffee house might be one moored on the Thames with a unique view of London, attractive ladies and men, good wine, a little music... pretty soon folk could be having a good time. Well...once upon a time...on 13th April 1668 to be exact, Pepys stayed at such a place (of course there were beds). Called a floating house of entertainment, Folly on The Thames, not surprisingly, was a huge success. In the early days a fashionable place for courtiers and their followers, even Queen Mary popped in to see what was going on. Later, in the words of a fun spoiler of the time 'It sank into a receptacle for companies of loose and disorderly people for purposes of drinking and promiscuous dancing'. This probably meant that poor folk were turning up and having fun. Well that would never do now would it? End of floating dream coffee house.

Flat white
Cold brew

COFFEE WAYS

by Marc Dietrich

Espresso
Small strong black coffee. Intensely aromatic, served in a tiny cup with a crown of golden brown froth called 'crema'. In Italy an espresso is often served with a twist of lemon peel.

Ristretto
A stronger version of espresso but with half the water.

Doppio or caffè doppio
A double espresso made with twice the coffee and twice the water.

Cappuccino
Equal amounts of espresso, steamed milk and foamed milk. This creates a thick cap of 'froth' that can have chocolate or cinnamon powder sprinkled on top of it. The name comes from the colour of the habit worn by the Capuchin monks.

Caffè latte
A contemporary American classic – hot steamed milk poured through espresso coffee – usually a double shot – and bigger than a cappuccino. Sprinkles added to taste.

Caffè macchiato
A one-shot espresso with a dash of foamed milk. The reverse – foamed milk with a dash of espresso, is called latte macchiato.

Caffè mocha
Hot chocolate poured through a two-shot espresso with flaked bitter-sweet chocolate on top.

Caffè viennois or mocha espresso
Creamy frothed milk with a generous dash of hot chocolate poured through a two-shot espresso – plus a head of whipped cream – usually served in a tall glass with a long spoon.

An ingredient that can work magic beyond you favourite drink. Adding depth & balancing sweetness [weak] Add teaspoon expresso/powder into choc cake - Brings out richness of choc. Mix ground coffee with crushed chillies paprika, brown sugar & oregano, use as a rub

A brief summary of
COFFEE & COFFEE BLENDING

by Mary Banks

Coffee is grown in over fifty countries, all within the tropical belt. The trees which produce coffee are in the genus *Coffea* which belongs to the *Rubiaceae* family. There are about fifty different species, though only two, the *Coffea arabica* and the *Coffea canephora* (usually called *robusta*) are commercially significant. *Coffea arabica* grows on steep slopes and plateaux, at heights between two and six thousand feet, while *robusta* grows well in the humidity of the equatorial forests from sea level to two thousand feet.

There are few visible differences between the two; *robusta* has larger, more corrugated leaves, a more vigorous growth pattern, is more resistant to disease, and has smaller, rounder beans. *Arabica*, though more delicate, accounts for about seventy five per cent of world production.

The Tree

A coffee tree starts to bear fruit when it is from three to five years old and if it survives pests, disease, droughts, floods, frosts and earthquakes may be fruitful for twenty five years. The tree is a typical evergreen shrub which in the wild may become thirty five feet high. In cultivation it is pruned to between six and ten feet. The fruit of one tree produces one to two pounds of processed coffee a year. The tree produces clusters of creamy-white blossoms, which look and smell like jasmine and last for about three days.

After self-pollination the berries develop, and as they grow change from green to deep red when they are known as 'cherries'. The coffee tree is one of those rare plants capable of producing blossoms, green-turning-to-yellow fruit, and mature red cherries all on the same branch.

Processing

The red skin of the cherry covers a sweet pulp which surrounds usually two coffee seeds, or beans. Each bean is covered with a thin husk called the parchment skin under which is another very thin, delicate layer called silver skin. The first task after picking the fruit is to remove all the layers of skin and pulp from the size-sorted coffee beans which are then dried, weighed, sacked, sold and shipped. If the purchaser is a large company the beans go from the docks to the factory where they are blended, roasted, ground and packaged. However many importers are suppliers who may sell sacks of green coffee beans directly to small roasters and specialist shops.

Blending
Many well known supermarket brands are a combination of coffees from several different countries, and even that described as from one country can be from different growths or regions within the country. There are three basic reasons for blending coffee:

- Flavour, aroma, body and colour. A high grown arabica may have excellent flavour but lack body and be thin in the cup. So a better drink might be obtained by adding a smaller proportion of a more neutral flavoured coffee which produces a heavier liquor. A third coffee may be added which has a particularly pleasant aroma. Like flowers which are beautiful but not fragrant, some coffees have very little aroma. Most coffees appear similar when served black but some look greyish when milk is added. So a fourth might be added to ensure a lovely tan or golden colour when a whitener is used.
- Price. Many high quality coffees if sold unblended would be too expensive for the average consumer. Through skillful blending and 'extending' the coffee with others, lower in price but less influential in the final flavour, blenders try to achieve quality with economy.
- Consistency. The amount of rainfall, hours of sunshine, harvesting conditions, processing, grading and storage will help determine the quality of a particular coffee. In certain regions frost or drought can be factors too. Companies can decrease their dependency on these variables by blending smaller amounts of coffee from more countries, so that if the price of one coffee should rise too much it can be replaced by a similar coffee from somewhere else without a discernible difference in taste. A commercial blend may consist of coffees from a dozen different countries.

No Taboos
Blending can be done before or after roasting, and any coffee can be blended with any other. If two coffees are blended the result may not taste like either, and with hundreds of coffees from around the world to choose from, the task of blending would be daunting without some guiding considerations.

Considerations
How, When, and Where are questions which when answered help determine what coffees may be desirable for a blend. How is the coffee going to be brewed and served? At what time of the day? What kind of

water is going to be used? Is there a traditional preferred taste already established there? These questions are not easily answered by the blender even when the destination of the coffee is known.

Roasting

Degrees of roast can alter the characteristics of any individual coffee. Various ways of brewing require various degrees of roast. For instance espresso requires a dark roast, though a lighter roast might be preferable if the coffee is to be brewed by another method, or drunk in the morning. If it is likely that the coffee will be drunk with milk, a light or medium roast will bring out the best characteristics of the coffee as the higher acidity will be neutralised by the alkaline of the milk, and a mild mellow flavour will come through. If the coffee is intended for after dinner or a heavier richer coffee is required, the blender may include a portion of *robusta* in the blend. Robusta coffees, which are generally at their best roasted quite dark, or dark roasted *arabicas* may produce a slightly bitter flavour, which can be off-set by a sweetener.

Water Used

This is a factor of great complexity, but in general the best natural water to use is slightly hard. Some blends will respond better than others to very hard or very soft water. Never use chemically softened water as the flavour will be greatly impaired.

Speciality Coffees

In many cases it is hard for large commercial blenders to consider regional water differences, particularly as they have limited control over the distribution of their products. This leaves room for the speciality shop owner who may develop a blend for the natural water of the region. The best of these can accommodate any individual taste or regional requirement with the vast array of speciality coffees at their disposal.

Additives

Some blends contain fig seasoning or chicory. By law a company should indicate the presence of these ingredients if they constitute more than 4 percent of the volume. In the United Kingdom blends containing fig are usually marketed as Viennese while those with chicory are designated French-Style. This doesn't mean that all coffee blended, roasted or packed in France contains additives.

Mary Banks worked in London for the International Coffee Organisation advising to the coffee trade. She is a freelance coffee consultant, speaker, trainer and taster.

ESPRESSO
and its origins
by Louie Salvoni

With virtually every Italian espresso machine manufacturer having claimed the credit for the espresso system at one time or another, it will probably come as a bit of a surprise to learn that the machine and method was originated by a Frenchman, one Louis Bernard Rabout, as long ago as 1822.

The principle, based upon the machine, of heating water to boiling inside a tank and letting steam gather at the top of the tank, then forcing the hot water through a straining device containing the coffee once a valve was opened below the water surface, was the same as that employed by the oldest café machines and that of the present home espresso brewer or stove-pots.

The idea was first put to commercial use by another Frenchman, Edward Loysel de Santais, some 21 years later. He produced a large café version, shown to the world at the 1855 Paris Exposition. By the turn of the century, thankfully, a few Italians modified Santais' machine, reducing the size of the strainer and increasing the number of valves to enable the brewing of several cups of coffee at the same time rather than a pot at a time. It was this speeding up of the operation that coined the term espresso.

The Italians took to the method with passion and it is now generally acknowledged that the modern café machine and caffè espresso method should be accredited to Luigi Bezzera who in 1902 patented the first machine. His company, run by his great grandson, Guido Bezzera, still manufactures espresso machines.

What is Espresso?

A concentrated coffee liquor, between 1.5 and 2 fluid ounces, made by forcing water at a temperature of between 93 and 96 degrees centigrade through a tightly compacted wad of finely ground, dark roasted coffee of between 6 and 7 grammes in weight per portion, and a brewing duration of 20 to 25 seconds. This is the basis for all coffee drinks.

Louie Salvoni is a partner in Brasilia Machines U.K.
This article first appeared in Esprit d'Espresso by Rolf Cornell and Steven Sullivan. We thank them and David Sullivan for allowing us to use it.

The Gourmet Coffee Club

*The Gourmet Coffee Club of London offers
its members speciality coffee of the highest quality
arabica beans, from the finest coffee growing regions
of the world. Members are guaranteed a selection of
original and special blended coffee at competitive
prices, and benefit from the experience of London's
most knowledgeable coffee connoisseurs and
professionals. If you enjoy the taste of real coffee
then you will be interested in the
Gourmet Coffee Club of London.*

*For our list of coffees and advantages to
club members write to:
4 Askew Mansions, Askew Road,
London W12 9DA
or telephone 0181 749 3102*

LONDON'S GOOD COFFEE SHOPS

EDUCATED PALATE

93 Kew Road, Richmond, Surrey TW9. 0181 940 0733
8am-6.30pm every day

This appears on first sight to be an exquisite traiteur, which is exactly what it is: Steven Arnold, the owner, uses many carefully selected distributors to offer the very best in cheeses, salamis, pâtés, fresh cooked meat, ready made hot dishes, pastries, cakes and freshly baked breads to his customers, as well as a wonderful range of gift-wrapped preserves, speciality oils, jams, Richmond honey and Neuhaus chocolates... the list could go on forever. But he also sells over-the-counter coffee beans, which can be sampled in a cosy mirrored room at the back of the shop, or at a marble counter overlooking the street. This is an ideal spot for a 'gourmet sandwich' and a continental blend espresso. Ina the manager would choose to go nowhere else in London for her coffee, and we could not argue. This shop is a 'Traiteur Superieur' in every sense of the word. And at weekends you can't move for regulars.

HOTHOUSE CAFE

9 Station Approach, Kew Gardens, TW9. 0181 332 1923
10am-7pm every day

Melanie, the owner, has created a cult in this cheery café with its pale ragged walls, bright blue lights, tables and seats. Taylor's of Harrogate coffee is served in every possible form, and flavoured coffees imported from New York are fast becoming popular. There is also a vast selection of herbal teas to choose from, and hot chocolate served in more ways than you ever thought possible. All this is also available to try at home, as at the back of the shop is a counter selling all these delicacies, adding Café Tasse fine chocolates to its list, as well as tea and coffee accessories. Upbeat music plays in the background, which adds a happy atmosphere in which to chat, read up-to-date papers, and drink the always excellent coffee in infinite ways. Just to add: you can drink alcohol with a selection of homemade hot and cold snacks, such as scrambled egg and smoked salmon, or speciality ciabatta sandwiches. Homemade soup here is excellent. This café has such a following that you can buy a Hothouse T-shirt for ten pounds, to advertise your appreciation.

EDUCATED PALATE
21 Barnes High Street, SW13. 0181 878 2041
9am-6pm every day

Sister to the Richmond traiteur, the emphasis here is on the café where comfortable colonial chairs are set at marble bistro tables. Delicate green paint and wrought iron work create shelves to line the walls, holding the carefully selected jams, vinegars, oils and gift wrapped preserves this continental traiteur is now so renowned for.

Amidst the contented local crowd of young mothers meeting for a chat, (safe in the knowledge that their children are happily catered for) stands the coffee bar and counter where all the action takes place. This is so laden with good things that to anyone remotely hungry it is like finding buried treasure: freshly cooked meats, cheeses, salamis, decadent patisseries, ready cooked meals, viennoiseries... all capturing your attention in a brightly lit display. In fact it is tempting to choose your

treats and run home to taste them, but on spotting the menu and the happy café customers you will want to eat immediately.

There are various breakfasts to set you up for the day and then a selection of sandwiches, salads, homemade soups and hot dishes take over at lunchtime. The patisseries should not be missed and with a long drinks list are well complemented, though cappuccinos are ordered every time here, chosen on their reputation.

In summer the doors open to extend the café onto the pavement and regulars stop to relax before or after their stroll along the river.

CYBERIA, EALING
73 New Broadway, W5. 0181 840 4123
Mon to Sat 11am-10pm   Sun 11am-9pm
A totally new experience is to be had in Ealing. It's refreshing, adventurous and exciting, bringing the spectacular world of the Internet within easy reach of everyone. If you are a complete technophobe no matter. Everyone is welcome and cyberhosts will lead you into the gallery of cyberspace. Specialised courses, including one at breakfast time, are available. Coffee and croissants in cyberia, anyone? The café is stylish with bold use of primary colours, flowers, lots of healthy plant life and imaginative lighting. Plenty of bright chairs at chrome tables. Along one wall are the work stations where you can perch on padded stools. Opposite is the café bar with the dishes of the day, and a myriad of Cyberia merchandise. Food is simple and excellent, with a seasonally changing menu all freshly prepared here. It may include home made pizzas and quiches, some vegetarian, soups and a variety of croissants and sandwiches. There are also great Greek cakes. Coffee is very good Segafredo. Cappuccino, espresso, filtered and decaf are on offer. Ask about the coffee of the day which might be with whipped cream, or various flavours such as almond or vanilla. So even if you don't wish to use a keyboard, just grab a coffee, read a paper and perhaps dream of other kinds of surfing.

THE OLD CHISWICK COFFEE HOUSE (BOHEME)
472 Chiswick High Road, W4.
Tues to Sat 10am-6.30pm   Sun-midday 6.pm
You could be forgiven for thinking that Peter Indic, the owner of this curiosity shop, inherited it through many generations past, for not only is its structure of 'listed building' quality, but every painting, object, relic, poster and piece of china also has a history that jumps out at you and makes you question its origins, as you sip a lovingly prepared coffee

and listen to soothing lute music through the gentle murmur of chatting fellow coffee drinkers. Well, actually, Peter and his wife opened this shop only three years ago, with the idea of designing a place where 'We would want to sit ourselves and read the paper over a good coffee'. So here it is: exactly that. There is a small menu of all the things you always want to eat, such as good viennoiseries, sandwiches and scrambled egg on toast. Plus a variety of ever-popular cakes, and when Peter extends into the basement and opens in the evenings as a restaurant, he will have more room for both his collection and his customers.

FOUBERT'S

162 – 168 Chiswick High Road, W4.   0181 994 5202
8.30am-11.30pm every day
This delightful Italian bar/restaurant can provide for all your needs. There is good coffee, home made ice cream, light or substantial food all day, a piano bar in the evening, and you can stay overnight.

CAFE DELICIEUX

220 King Street, Hammersmith W6.   0181 563 2930
Tues to Fri 8am-8pm   Sat & Mon 10am-8pm   Sun 10am-4pm
Ever dream in that warm haze, just before you wake, of having coffee in a family run, French country café? Keep your eyes shut a few moments longer, between sips munch an extremely delectable pain au chocolat half the size of your pillow. Hmm…dream on. The friendly proprietor, wearing a beret, hands you a paper, a charming girl brings some soup. You sip. It is divine. Beside you the beautiful woman of earlier dreams encourages you to try a mouthful of scrambled eggs, which seem to float in your mouth. You glance at the paper. Strangely it is in English and bears today's date. There are pictures of snowdrifts in Scotland. You ask for the bill. It is so small you fear a mistake but they smile and say no. You and your beautiful companion leave. Outside you shiver and hug in the dank gloom. Look back at the friendly light. Notice on the glass door the address: 220 King Street. You know that when you awake it will be gone... It hasn't gone! In fact it is booming. The proprietor, Alain Collignon has been in England some years and this is his first restaurant. He trained at the famous Gaston Le Nôtre in Paris, and nearly everything here is made by him from English ingredients. Word is now spreading so fast about Alain's culinary delights that he is offering take away, birthday cakes to order and his happy café for any 'bring your own' occasion you can think of.

OPORTO

22a Hammersmith Broadway, W6.   0181 563 9744
7am-8pm every day

At a recent gathering in the city, conversation turned to the mystery of Disney buying Hammersmith Broadway. Several theories were put forward without much conviction until somebody said that he'd been to Gaz's the night before and been told that Disney's top banana Michael Eisner who pays himself 250 million a year (give or take the odd 100 mill.) and therefore probably knows a thing or two, put out the small change because he wants to be sure of a good cup of coffee when he gets to London and that's where Tony da Silva's is. So we hurry on down there and Tony da Silva turns out to be none other than Tony from Oporto on Golborne Road, which is where coffee was discovered in Notting Hill. Well Disney hit the mother lode alright, or at least a direct line to Portugal. Tony is from Oporto (Tony calls all his places Oporto in order to make things easy to remember) by way of Sintra and believes in the local products. He uses Buondi coffee, which is excellent, and his bakery turns out traditional Portuguese pastries. Pasteis de Nata and Bolo di Arroz are legendary. So if you find yourself in Hammersmith don't miss this place.

SUTHERLANDS

140 Shepherd's Bush Road, W6.   0171 603 5717
8.30am-about 6pm every day

John Sutherland was having such success with this delicatessen that he decided to 'Give the buyer a break' literally, and opened a coffee shop in the back. Two years on, he is amazed how well it's doing and how much he enjoys what worried him most about the move...making coffee for discerning customers. He needn't have worried. He uses his own mixture of beans and the coffee really is good. While you sit here, pondering pleasant possibilities from the shop, you may as well keep your strength up with some examples. There are delicacies from pinenut oil to poppyseed bread, (and many other fresh loaves) fine preserves and Parma ham. Homemade cakes are especially appealing, as are the cheeses and...well better perhaps to just see for yourself. And whilst there, take time to enjoy the current exhibition: these are the talents of regular customers – artists happily being given the chance to be shown.

OPORTO PATISSERIE

461 – 465 North End Road, SW6. 0171 385 5002
8am-8pm every day

Just off Fulham Road opposite Safeway. These pinpoint but uninspiring directions didn't prepare us for the exotic Brazilian touch Alan Dall'Agnol has given this café. Oporto's freshness and spacious relaxed feel, with its beautiful green tiled floor, are as attractive as the excellent Portuguese delicacies to be found here. The coffee is good, 'Italian sounding but really Brazilian' Alan points out, as he darts in to check progress and get a quick fix between visits to several other businesses he has on the boil around here. They will make your coffee however you wish so be sure to tell them exactly how you like it. There are lots of traditional Portuguese pastries such as Pasteis de Nata, as well as good continental patisseries, and with a little warning, Oporto will cater for anything from a picnic to a wedding.

CULLENS PATISSERIE

108 Holland Park Avenue, W11.   0171 221 3598
8am-8pm every day

Part of Holland Park Avenue 'Village', and set next to its own grocery store, and the famous Lidgate Butchers, this warmly lit café with its Art Deco feel offers you generous cups of Musetti coffee from a Brasilia machine, served also as Latte and in cafetières (with various teas on offer too). Papers are to hand as you settle down in the comfortable red padded chairs and benches set snugly up against the warm wood/ mirrored walls, and contemplate the menu: a sophisticated mix of light snacks including mezze, jacket potatoes, quiche, soup, various speciality sandwiches and breakfasts which are served from 8am to midday. All this couldn't be mentioned if no room is left to try the meticulously created cakes, pastries, and viennoiseries which are displayed along the length of the counter from the entrance of the shop and are sold often to people who use Cullens as their regular bakery/patisserie (and everything looks superb). Jazz /piano music gives a Continental café feel and, dare I say it, could allow you to think of Paris or Vienna if your imagination is really working.

ARGILE GALLERY *Café*

7 Blenheim Crescent, W11.   0171 792 0888
Tues to Fri 11am-6pm   Sat 10am-6pm

A beautiful painter from Lebanon, Marie Saba started this gallery in the eighties. When things slowed up a bit around here, she put in some

tables and chairs and transformed it into what may be the most
enjoyable place in London to see paintings. It is certainly one of the
most enjoyable places in London to savour a good cup of coffee. Marie's
husband, Nabil is a famous Middle Eastern artist, and when you have
checked what's on the walls, you can amuse yourself by going through
his cartoon book, Face the Facts. In fact, between cups you could go
through several books, as Argile is across from Books for Cooks, and
almost next to the Travel Bookshop. If you can't decide whether to
travel, or cook don't worry, just settle in and have lunch. Some of
Marie's Mediterranean dishes are so delicate that you won't want to
travel and you certainly won't need to cook. The lime cheesecake is
particularly good to dream on. With some dishes there is a free glass
of wine or you can bring your own bottle.

CAFE DIANA

5 Wellington Terrace, W2.   0171 792 9606

7am-5.30pm every day

Heading towards Kensington Palace Gardens from either direction, there is a distinct landmark to be taken into account; it's not actually Kensington Palace itself but a small coffee shop directly opposite the gates, and it is no surprise to find that this is Princess Diana's local coffee stop where she will pop in for a great coffee, a chat, and a bite to eat. Abdul the owner has fittingly hung his walls with the most stunning photos of the Princess looking beautiful and radiant. There are two heartwarming pictures of her with him and his helpers. Well...the coffee, Drury, is served by connoisseurs who offered us a short pick you up espresso...excellent, though cappuccino is the more popular form. A selection of teas and chocolate are served too. There is a large and varied breakfast menu which attracts a full house all morning, then Abdul's famous pitta bread sandwiches. Falafel and Kofta kebabs (all meat being cooked on an open flame grill) take over from lunchtime. Tempting desserts are on offer too. When Abdul finally manages to expand into the back room and serve food into the evenings with an alcohol licence (neighbour allowing) this will be good news for customers and Abdul's friend the Princess of Hearts.

THE CAFE GROVE

255 Portobello Road, W11.   0171 243 1094

May to Aug 9am-11pm   Sun 10.30am-5.30pm

Sept to April 9am-5pm   Sun 10.30am-5.30pm

Ross and Luigi, the owners, built this café literally brick by brick, nail by nail, from a derelict building into the vibrant cosmopolitan place it is today. Enter the café through an inconspicuous door in this busy part of Portobello, and ascend a spiral stair to the first floor. Here you find high quality coffee enthusiastically served by people interested in your welfare, along with a mouthwatering selection of food: anything from a simple croissant to excellent Mexican, Mediterranean or other exotic dishes, depending on the cook's inspiration of the moment. Just relax here with a newspaper, or have one of the great weekend treats of London by having breakfast out on the balcony and watching the most bustling street market in London come to life.

CHERRIES

3 Chepstow Road, W2. 0171 221 9253

7am-midnight every day

The first place to be a delicatessen and a coffee shop – Cherries has become an institution here. It is long and clean and sparse but comfortable, like an E.U. dining car, with a counter area at the entrance end where one can view and purchase all manner of delicious necessities neatly and sensibly presented to lay claim to both the salt and sugar receptors of the tongue and which then gives gently but decidedly away to a more extended area of tables and chairs. What seems to have been an initial attempt to effect some semblance of a pan-Mediterranean decorative motif, sparse and with clear glass running the full length of it has, mercifully, stopped so that what remains is a true minimalist feeling, unforced, unobtrusive. The coffee and the baguettes are simple and delicious. The man who runs the place is lean and Latin and is in constant motion. He runs a tight ship lording over what may very well be the greatest secret to his success, the delightful group of semi sullen, semi ironic, semi blond, semi brunette, smirking, no nonsense, and frankly very sexy young Yugoslav/Spanish women who take all the orders and who keep the excellent coffee flowing. The owner's other great secret is his ability to limit any contagion of his own manic pace. His energies are devoted entirely to the establishment's success and he is well aware that a key element in that success is the feeling all of its patrons have of not being in any way rushed. They know they can hang out as long as they wish.

THE COURTYARD CAFE

59a Portobello Road, W11. 0171 221 8416

Tues to Fri 9am-5pm   Sat 10am-5pm

This place is a joy. One of the great hidden treats of London, it also does some real good in the local community. It is set back in a small pretty courtyard, with greenery to look at through twelve foot high French windows (you can sit out there too). Wooden floors, sturdy tables with stout wooden chairs and some church pews set off the pretty, ragged lemon walls. Upstairs on the small balcony it is possible to have a very private chat while relaxing in the comfort of wicker chairs. The policy here is to look after the local people especially well, to make visitors just as welcome, and to make an oasis of peace that one can visit on one's own. The filter coffee may be the best value in London, while the espresso machine steams out plenty of the real thing at normal prices. Soup is a special bargain, and there are many fine homemade cakes and light dishes at great prices. St Peter's is a charity and the people who run it are charming, all volunteers. You won't want to leave.

FAT RASCALS

52 Ledbury Road, W11. 0171 792 8843

Mon to Sat 9am-6pm   Sun 10am-3pm

Fat Rascals are actually scone-like buns originating in Yorkshire, though I am happy to say that here, the quirky name is synonymous with something altogether more original. Wendy, a Roux brothers trained chef, has created a pad in which to sample (as they hover under your very nose) the most mouthwatering tarts, sandwiches, crostini and viennoiseries around. We drooled over the fresh, colourful and hunky Mediterranean style sandwiches all made on the premises, whilst debating whether or not to stay till lunch to taste the hot dish of the day. The great bread is sliced generously for toast which is a popular favourite with regulars, who, sitting at homely and eclectic wooden tables, spread it generously with luscious looking homemade jam from Bonne Maman type jars.

All this in communicative surroundings, where locals pin ads to the walls which range from yoga classes to houses to let and flyers for shows. They tend to be actors, models, individuals who have been drawn to an individual atmosphere. Their work is often displayed on the walls in the form of patterned iron work, mirrors etc. Oh, and by the way, the coffee is roasted down the road by the Coffee Store on Portobello Road and made on an Italian Machine, so could not be fresher. Teas and chocolate are available too. This little café does so well in fact that Wendy has it in mind to move into other areas too. Watch this space.

LISBOA

57 Golborne Road W10. 0181 968 5242

8am-8pm every day

For years Lisboa was simply 'the place' for anyone within miles of here who wanted a good cup of coffee. In the morning they always seem to open in top gear and quickly serve the waiting throng their fix. This is simply because they turn their machines on forty minutes before opening time so that the steam is well and truly up.

For some reason the denizens here seem to be superhuman, and you are likely to see some of them sitting out on ironwork chairs even on the most freezing day in winter, presumably shooting the breeze, or perhaps seeking a naturally iced coffee. Anyway the coffee is amazing. You don't have to sit out, but will want to in summer. The things to eat here are wonderful too: Pasteis de nata, Bolo de arroz, Faijao, and have such a reputation that cafés all over London are clamouring to stock them. Lisboa café and its Portuguese deli opposite are well worth crossing London for, and scores of people do.

MANZARA

24 Pembridge Road, W11. 0171 727 3062
Mon to Sat 8am-11.30pm   Sun 10am-10.30pm

Sergio the owner of this, one of the first restaurants to be also a coffee shop, has been so successful that few can ever hope to attain his standards. Professionalism is everything here, and Sergio can't understand how anybody could possibly want to buy in their pastries, or indeed survive in the business doing so. Almost everything is baked downstairs. The preparation starts at 11.30pm and when the head chef arrives each morning he starts to make the wonders for the day. Sergio, Turkish born, came to this country after a long stint in Paris, where he worked at some great places. You will get some idea of his reputation if you are a weekend visitor to Portobello, when you see people lining up to buy croissants from the huge mound in the window. The food at Manzara is wonderful, and what we took to be the entire restaurant

menu, in colour, turned out to be just the coffee menu which includes: Turkish Coffee, Espresso Romano, Espresso Borgia, Espresso iced, Cappuccino Latino, Cappuccino Francaise, Café Kioki and many more and we aren't going to tell you what they are in order not to spoil the fun of trying them for yourself.

MARNIES

9 Portobello Road, W11. 0171 229 8352

Mon to Sat 7.45am-4.30pm

This part of Portobello Road is where the trek to the markets on Saturdays begins in earnest, so it may be a good place to take a break if that's where you are bound – if you can get in the door that is, as regulars at Marnies know that they need to be alert if they aren't going to miss a seat at this interesting place, and quick off the mark they are. Marnie, a New Zealander, decorated the place herself, an obvious labour of love. The soft beige walls have been ragged and varnished to give some life. The skirtings restored to their original size from stunted sixties versions, and painted panelling gives depth. Marnie's eye for these things is classical, as a poster of Pompeii hints at. The coffee is excellent, and lots of good things are cooked downstairs. Mostly they don't have formal names and are whatever Marnie feels like doing. But one of the things that certainly does have a name and a big following is the cheesecake. Beyond a pretty window which fills the back of the shop can be seen happy, satisfied fans of Marnies taking their ease in the sun.

OPORTO PATISSERIE

68a Golborne Road W10. 0181 968 8839

8am-8pm every day

On the opposite side of the road to Lisboa, Oporto opened some years later and was an instant success. Partly because the owners were so nice, partly because any Portuguese café would have got instant attention with Lisboa and its reputation close by. But mostly because it was good. Another thing that is really good here is the light in the morning, especially if you like to read the newspaper with your coffee, which is great: espresso, cappuccino or coffee with lots of hot milk in a large glass – Galao – to be really Portuguese. And if you like it stronger the word is Maya Fort. The pastries and sandwiches are excellent. Through the day there is an interesting series of inhabitants: first the early morning newspaper readers. A bit later, the first flush of Portuguese and Spanish people who feel at home here. Mid morning sees teachers and pupils from the adult school around the corner, then the script writers, before the Portuguese take it back again. And if you go to Mass on Sundays at the local church, Oporto is the place to meet up with your friends afterwards.

CAFE Q.E.L.

The Old Queen Elizabeth Laundry,
5 Ladbroke Road, W11. 0171 221 7936
Mon to Fri 9.30am-6pm   Sat 9am-6pm   Sun 10am-6pm

Tucked just around the corner from Notting Hill Gate tube on the way to (or from) Portobello Road, with its original 1890's sign boarding still intact, is the Queen Elizabeth Laundry. But please don't be fooled into bringing your washing here, for this is now a little haven for coffee and chocolate lovers alike. Warwick de Winter, the genial Dutch owner, ran this shop as an antiques business until he realised the desperate need locally for a good continental pavement café. So nearly two years ago, with much help and enthusiasm, he transformed the place into its present attractive continental atmosphere. His natural enthusiasm meant that the nectar he had found in Veronese cafés had to be tapped. And he succeeded: a strong Italian roast is imported directly from Verona, along with the most delectable hot chocolate ever tasted – heaven sent. With a strong slant on Dutch/Indonesian specialities, (a Dutch breakfast – uitsmijter – is on the menu, as well as fricandel) and irresistible homemade soups, cakes and Italian-baked bread and viennoiseries, it is a simple pleasure to sit here, in summer out on the busy terrace, or at any time inside at cheerfully covered tables amongst plants and memorabilia, sipping coffee and dreaming of piazzas, pizzas, Pisa...

TOM CONRAN'S DELI AND CAFE

226 Westbourne Grove, W11.   0171 221 8818
Mon to Sat 8am-8pm   Sun 10am-4pm

Tom Conran's delicatessen is firmly at the W11 end of Westbourne Grove, opposite the classiest public conveniences in London. It is part of a clutch of specialist shops – antiques, clothing, jewellery and flowers, as well as an award-winning wholefoods centre – that runs into the top end of the Saturday market on Portobello Road. Amongst the cheeses, salamis and prettily packaged goods in the delicatessen there is always a spread of little sweet or savoury tarts, delicious cakes, and ready-prepared dishes to take away by the pound. These can now be eaten in the recently opened café, shedding the frustration of having to get home before sinking your teeth into them. The café itself is small – seven marble topped tables with sherbet-orange painted chairs, kindergarten style except in size, gathered around them. There is a daily lunch menu from 1pm to 4pm, (minimum charge £5) of colourful dishes – some leafy, some noodley, some seared or chargrilled – and, of course, there are the tartelettes, cakes and pastries to choose from. 'There is every kind of coffee' according to the confident waitress, and judging by the queues for take away cappuccino, everyone in the area knows it's good. Tom's Café is a light little burst for the tastebuds, perfect for a delicious quick lunch or a hot caffè latte on the hop, and in warm weather the pretty country gardens at the back allow you to linger in quiet seclusion for a while, though with Portobello down the road, who needs to?

BYZANTIUM

31 Moscow Road, W2.   0171 229 9367
9am-11pm every day

After you pass this place a few times you just have to go in to see the beautiful old brass coffee machine which takes your eye from the street. A pleasantly exotic atmosphere greets you. Sit at marble topped tables, among people made even more interesting in the mirrored wall which makes the place seem twice its size. There are excellent savouries and milk shakes made with Haagen-Dazs. The coffee is excellent and people wanting a memory of Greece come here for frappés, and traditional savouries and sweets. The bazaar atmosphere is augmented by lively radio which only seems incongruous once your ears work out that it's Capital which has been chosen as a compromise from the earlier classical and Greek music stations. Byzantium is extremely popular and is beautifully run by the glamourous owner who permits no football or political argument here. Byzantium has a large following of regular customers.

PIERRE PECHON PATISSERIE

127 Queensway W2.   0171 229 0746
Mon to Wed 7am-7pm   Thur to Sat 7am-8pm   Sun 7.30am-7pm

On a wet January morning, make one's way up Queensway, ignoring several beckoning eateries, push through a crowded bakery into a brightly lit café at the back. Order coffee from a welcoming waiter, and sit feeling warm and happy knowing that at least someone in this bleak world cares about you. A glance at the paper reassures that Prince Harry is doing well on his ski board, whatever that is. Coffee is excellent. Check the menu. Happy to read that they serve English breakfast extensive enough for denizens of country houses of Edwardian times, or

any truck driver of any time, all the way to 3pm. Order what is known by one and all to be one of the best croissants in town. They've been at this since 1925, and haven't served a bad one yet. Paper now telling where a lady has come back from the dead, or at least from the mortuary where the doctor sent her. Wish that one day some doctor can be that wrong about me, and see sadly that the scales have already evened things up a bit...Lincoln Kerstein has died and at time of going to press shows no signs of making it a revival meeting. Back to the menu to disguise an interest in the cheery, bubbling conversations going on in several languages, some even may be in English. Caught neatly by heading 'Highlights and Addictions' cleverly put there to catch weak creatures. Order pancakes with honey and lemon. Trying to remember what the day outside is like. See a sad bedraggled wet lady come in, looks instantly twenty years happier on being warmly greeted by the waiter. Catch his eye, add to the pancake, an ' ice cream of any flavour'.

BAZZICA

14 St Albans Grove, W8. 0171 795 6467

Mon to Fri 8am-6.30pm   Sat 12pm-6pm

Bazzica means 'a place to hang out', and if you want a really quiet place in Kensington, here it is. Come to think of it you probably aren't going to find a more restful place in London. Tucked away between High Street Kensington and Gloucester Road, this is where regulars from Leith's cooking school meet regulars from the Carpenters Arms and students from the American College. Coffee is excellent – Lavazza – the customers' choice, and with Bouquillon patisseries before your very eyes can rarely be taken without an accompanying pastry to make you feel right with the world. And to ring the changes, try your coffee iced or flavoured with syrup. For those feeling health conscious, fresh fruit and vegetable juices are pressed to order to create a choice of combinations – courgette, celery and carrot juice surely giving you an above average supply of betacarotene – and with pirosky and salt beef sandwiches on the menu, this café is attracting more and more happy customers to its tables, which in the warm summer months spill out onto the peaceful street corner, just a stone's throw away from the crowds.

CAFE PASTA

229/231 Kensington High Street W8.   0171 937 6314

Mon to Sat 9am-11.30pm   Sun till 11pm

Café Pasta has already had an award from the government for Investors in People which may help to explain why the pleasant atmosphere about this continental style café starts to make you feel welcome even before you walk in. This is partly because so many people seem to be enjoying themselves outside, where the café spills onto the street, making you want to feel as happy as they look, and partly because the staff are well trained and are happy to make your life happy. There are fresh flowers and pictures all over the walls and there is so much life coming and going, that you will feel part of the human race whatever your mood was on arriving. A remarkable number of people from all walks of life obviously treat this place as home base. Here you can have anything you want at any time of the day from the coffee and snack menu, or the main Pasta menu. There are papers to read, excellent coffee, or as the café is fully licensed you can have just a glass of wine.

There is wheelchair access. High chairs and colouring pages are provided for children.

Other branches:

270 Chiswick High Road, W4. 0181 995 2903

8 High Street, Wimbledon, SW19. 0181 944 6893

PAGLIACCI COFFEE SHOP

1 Argyll Road, W8. (By Safeways) 0171 795 6788

8am-6pm every day (later in Summer)

There is a warm and spacious feel to this elegant coffee shop, enhanced
by burnt copper coloured tables and chairs, deep orange coloured menus
and a spotlessly clean copper counter. Mo, the owner, is a true coffee
lover and has tasted and re-tasted every kind of coffee roast, and tested
every coffee distributor and every coffee machine available in this
country. The result is a constantly superb Musetti coffee, from a sophisticated and beautifully maintained Faema machine, served in as many
ways as you could wish. In fact this shop is getting regulars from all over
the area, which is no surprise, since the delectable cakes, consistently
popular grilled ciabatta, delicious panini, Musetti hot chocolate and the
ever delicious coffee mean Pagliacci's is fast becoming famous...added to
this, the large terrace practically doubles the size of the café in hotter
weather and Mo plays Italian opera and classical music which greets you
on arrival, making you feel like a king as soon as you walk into this
wonderful atmosphere. Don't be the last person to discover it!

PIERRE PECHON PATISSERIE

27, Kensington Church Street, W8. 0171 937 9574

Mon to Sat 8am-6pm

This outpost of the great bakery set up in Queensway early this century
is a favourite around here with hosts of regulars of all ages. The four
tables are constantly busy with an exotic mix of Kensington people in
the know as it is just far enough up Church Street to be missed by the
mass of shoppers. 'It's nice working here as so many customers feel we
are part of their life.' It is also a great favourite with children who
especially like the baked animals. A long time contender for best bakery
in town, Pechon goes into overdrive at Easter especially providing for the
Greek community. The coffee is good and since one visit creates an
addict you'll need the antidote to Pechon: across the street a slit takes
you into Kensington gardens where you can pleasantly stroll it all off,
between pauses to munch of course.

FLEUR DE LYS

13a Gloucester Road, SW7. 0171 589 4045

7.30am-6.30pm every day

When Tamas Lorrant retired, lots of people at the BBC's Bush House,
and other regulars of Rendezvous on Regent Street, mourned the loss of
a great restaurateur. What he did in retirement caused coffee drinkers

around Kensington to mourn the end of a great coffee spot when he died two years ago. They didn't need to. Though Fleur de Lys isn't the same without Tamas, a Hungarian, it is as close to being the same as Enid, his Geordie wife, can keep it. The coffee is the same. A really good continental for espresso and cappuccino. Good patisseries, as well as breakfast from 7.30 each morning, light lunches, Ciabatta sandwiches and, of course, Baps. Their own Fleur de Lys blend is on sale to take away, in beans or ground, as well as Brazilian Santos, Costa Rica, Continental, or Mocha Mysore for the many around here who make Turkish coffee.

BALANS – WEST

239 Old Brompton Road, Earls Court SW5. 0171 244 8838
8am-2am every day   Licensed
Fronted by bay trees and capacious brown canopies, this is a superb venue, just a couple of minutes away from the tube.

Style and elegance are the order of the day here, coupled with a tremendously friendly, welcoming atmosphere. The decor is contemporary, with tables and chairs arranged and designed by Conran. A feeling of light and space prevails, helped by a gorgeous American maple floor and delightfully large windows looking out onto the street life of Earl's Court. Running almost the entire length of one wall is a sumptuous banquette, just begging to be sat on. There's also a conservatory, creating a slightly more intimate environment, and for balmier days, a secluded patio.

At the centre of operations is a marvellous burnished aluminium bar near to which all the exquisite food is freshly prepared. A blackboard highlights the specials of the day; or if you care to, choose from a gloriously varied menu. The range is mouth watering and includes oriental style vegetables on noodles, salmon and crab cakes, and eggs florentine.

The enthusiastic staff also serve a great cup of coffee. So just unwind here and sample the range that includes cappuccino, café au lait, filter, espresso, mocha and liqueur coffee.

TROUBADOUR

265 Old Brompton Road, SW5. 0171 370 1434
10am-11pm every day
One of the best known cafés in London, Troubadour was started by Michael van Bloemen who came to London from Canada in the early 1950s, looked around a little, pronounced the words of a recent hero of

the time 'I shall return', went back home for a few years to earn some
money, and just like General MacArthur, kept his word to the natives.
The music café he set up changed the course of many London lives.
The roof of this place is hung with every conceivable sort of small
stringed musical instrument, yes there's probably a grimy Strad up there
somewhere, which points to Michael's passion. Over the years there
have been some great performances downstairs, and Michael just shrugs
and laughs merrily about his impresario days. Even Bob Dylan's visits
were taken in stride and Michael's memories of him are personal rather
than musical. Michael retired to Dubrovnik and takes living in a war
zone in his stride too. However he visits London often and stays where
he always did – at the Troubadour. Events here include regular poetry
readings. A recent memorable short run of the play Bloody Poetry
threatens to reappear by popular demand. The person looking as
though he pays the winner of the lottery out of his own pocket is the
'new owner' Bruce who's only had the place twenty years. His only
thoughts are for your welfare and whether the prized and ancient coffee
machine will keep churning out great coffee or need another repair job
from the sort of maintenance man who retired forty years ago. There
aren't as many of these about as there were, hence Bruce's worried look.
In those challenging words of the theatre 'this one's unmissable'.

CAFFE NERO

66 Old Brompton Road, SW7.   0171 589 1760

Mon to Fri 7am-9pm   Sat & Sun 8am-9pm

Cool, clean, efficient and friendly, Caffè Nero is one of the new breed
of coffee bars destined as much for the urban professional as the passing
tourist. The interior appearance is post-industrial chic with galvanised
steel surfaces, marble and just enough black to reflect its name and any
customers with a vestigial nostalgia for the Roaring Eighties. High-level
counters and tables encourage standing and keep traffic moving quickly
inside, though pavement furniture allows for more leisurely people-
watching in the summer. Cappuccinos and espressos are of high quality
and good value, dark and full-flavoured without bitterness. A variety of
other coffees, including ristretto, café latte, iced and flavoured are
available. There is a good range of breakfast pastries: croissants, pains au
chocolat and sugar drenched churros are all baked on the premises; at
lunchtime, pizzas, imaginative rolls and pastas. Italian cakes are always
available for those with very sweet teeth. The attractive young staff clad
in black Caffè Nero tee shirts and jeans are an aesthetic bonus and the
three other branches are ideally situated in Soho, Covent Garden and
Regent Street for shoppers and business people alike. In June Nero opens
in Hampstead at 1 High Street between Whistles and Monsoon.

CROMWELL'S

23 Cromwell Place, SW7. 0171 584 8839

Mon to Fri 7am-7pm   Sat & Sun 8am-7pm

As you wander down from the Victoria and Albert Museum to South
Kensington tube station with your head still full of the priceless treasures
just seen, you suddenly realise that you're a little foot-sore and weary, and
your mind turns to the hope of discovering a cosy spot to stop and pep
yourself up with a good strong coffee...well, turn just a few steps right
into Cromwell Place and before your eyes is one of the cheeriest coffee
shops in the area, inviting you in to enjoy a special blend of espresso
coffee known only to Cromwells themselves: nectar! There is also a vast
selection of sandwiches made to order as well as many hot homemade
specials of the day such as Shepherds Pie and Lasagne, plus a choice of
great homemade soups and jacket potatoes worth queuing for. (Cakes
and patisseries are yet another temptation.) Added to this, the natural
wicker chairs, vibrant posters and paintwork and cosy balcony upstairs
all contribute to a very welcome discovery – a happy spot indeed.

FILERIC CAFE PATISSERIE

57 Old Brompton Road, SW7.   0171 584 2967

Mon to Sat 8am-8pm   Sun 9am-8pm

If you're a Francophile and regularly take trips to France to calm your withdrawal symptoms, then let Eurostar, passports, ferries, airports and luggage etc. drift into the dim and distant past. Here is France. And I defy you to find one iota of evidence to the contrary (with the exception, perhaps, of the use of Costa coffee, Twinings tea and a few English speaking regulars). From the charming French helpers, to the shop window and counter laden with sumptuous, totally French patisseries, (such as featherweight milles feuilles; 'Eden', a dark chocolate mousse/caramel and white chocolate mousse gateau, and a myriad choice of tartelettes and seasonal specialities such as Galette des Rois) cast your eyes around the small, cosy room to the 'marks' on the shelves: Teisseire; Lu; BN; mousseline; Bonne Maman... long-lost treats. So, treat yourself. It will certainly save you a journey and a few pounds which could be put to good use here.

RAISON D'ETRE

18 Bute Street, SW7.   0171 584 5008

Mon to Fri 7.30am-6pm   Sat 8.30am-6pm   Sun 9.30am-4pm

In the middle of London's French quarter has appeared a bright new coffee shop decorated simply and cleverly: a large single-paned window invites you into a warmly lit café, with a natural pine floor and cane chairs complementing the shiny chrome tables and Rancilio coffee machine. Consistently good Angelucci coffee is served which brings locals-in-the-know back for more. As well as good quality sandwiches and Delice de France bread and viennoiseries baked on the spot, there are great raclette baguettes and toasted focaccia (the house specialities) which are already reaching taste buds far and wide... P.S. Look closely at the walls!

HARRODS

Knightsbridge SW1.   0171 730 1234

Mon, Tues & Sat 10am-6pm   Wed, Thurs & Fri 10am-7pm

First freezing of winter, miserable day late January. Enter Harrods to meet a friend for coffee. Wander through ground floor to the cosmetics department to sniff things. Here in midmorning, lady in evening dress plays on the harp George Gershwin's Embraceable You. Gershwin must be chuckling somewhere. The day seems better already. Pass on through men's stuff to the stairs where one pauses to contemplate the plaque to

Harrodians who perished in the Great War and, of the hundred and forty nine, pick at random Edward Exton from removals and Henry Harvey from the meat department to say their names aloud so that someone passing may hear of them these eighty years on. Through luggage on 2nd floor, asking Amanda the way to coffee shop, still getting lost; into the book department which is so great I may never leave. Manage to find Café Harrods. Warm wood area with vibrant music and happy waiters, serving good coffee from colourful Mediterranean china. Realise I should be at Terrace Bar so head on up there, to where my friend is waiting.

Here high up on the terracotta facade of the building, hangs the most elegant other worldly conservatory, where charming waiters bring coffee as we gaze over the Knightsbridge roof tops and watch the snow softly falling to the gentle piano music from next door. We leave, heading out through the food halls which, along with a million other things, set Harrods apart from other coffee shops. Here we check to see that people wanting their haunch of venison tonight won't suffer disappointment, nor indeed those wishing for quail, or partridge with grey legs or red. Make sure the citizens tucking into their oysters are satisfied, or on the way to satisfaction, then check the silos for any new coffee that may have shown up on the planet, as this is obviously where it would be. Check too that the price of Blue Mountain hasn't moved from its overnight £30 per pound. Discuss coffee with Frances who makes up a new blend for us. We leave by the West door to see the Harrods wagon with its flowing tailed black horses drive by. The snow has made the day mild.

HARVEY NICHOLS 5TH FLOOR CAFE

109 Knightsbridge SW1. 0171 823 1839

Mon to Sat 10am-10.30pm   Sun noon-6.30pm

Emerge from the underground at Knightsbridge at almost any time of the day and chances are that you will notice a stream of attractive people heading in the direction of Harvey Nichols. Under the roof, in the Fifth Floor Café, is the liveliest meeting place in London, and one of the most fashionable, where you can enjoy yourself from morning till night. Get your coffee here in the morning as many regulars do, sit inside or out on the terrace, read a newspaper, then contemplate the myriad of possibilities. There is a flower market, a chocolate shop, a first class wine shop, a really good restaurant, a popular bar, and a tantalising market, stocked by Mark Lewis with foods from around the world, many of which can only be found here. At the coffee bar you can try the different blends which are exclusive to Harvey Nichols. They include Brazil Lagoa, Yauco Selecto from Puerto Rico and a Colombia Estate as well as one from Papua New Guinea. They will also make up a special blend just for you. Just in case all this isn't enough you can sit back and enjoy live jazz here in the evenings.

MINEMA CAFE BAR

43 Knightsbridge, SW1.   0171 823 1269

Mon to Fri 9am-9pm   Sat 10am-9pm   Sun noon-7pm

Looking for that clean, minimal Italian bar that London tries so hard to imitate without ever quite managing to? Look no further: seemingly displayed in a vast pane of glass on two levels, this café is designed almost entirely in chrome as it curves and corners its way into shapes such as revolving doors, bar stools, counters, chairs and table tops. Greenery stands happily in every spare corner, whilst magazines and papers from all over the world (*Le Monde*; the *Herald Tribune*; *Die Zeit* to name but a few) adorn the surfaces, and blackboards display a cross section of the world's taste in food and drink, ranging from sandwiches such as pastrami and sauerkraut on rye, to feta and tomato salad, homemade soup of the day, and Maison Blanc patisseries. On the ground floor where the action happens, alcohol is licensed from 11am, and regulars relax at the bar over a fresh fruit daiquiri or two. Upstairs at clever tables of ceramic slabs of marble, meals are served with alcohol. This is also an ideal spot to catch a short espresso whilst exchanging eye level glances with passing travellers on the top of the no's 19, 22, 74... double deckers as they crawl into Knightsbridge, or stretching your gaze further on to the joggers in the Park. In warm weather, the Minema Café can take you even nearer to the Park when the bar extends onto the pavement. At the same time you can enjoy a special offer of a meal, bottle of wine and a cinema ticket for an all-in price. (Cigarettes are sold too, and though the great china won't go unnoticed it knows where it belongs!...)

PATISSERIE VALERIE

215 Brompton Road, SW3.   0171 823 9971
Mon to Sat 7.30am-10.30pm   Sun 9am-6.30pm

The three Scalzo brothers have done the impossible: transplanted a legendary Soho café to Knightsbridge and made it even better than the original. In fact they've set new standards for every café to try for. From the moment you step into this place you know that everything's going to be all right. Very much an Arts Café, there is always something interesting on the walls and around the place. There are openings every few weeks and places are fought for by contemporary artists. The Matisse lithographs in April '96 and the Kandinsky influenced Easter

eggs are exciting visitors this spring. The atmosphere is so alive and so varied that it takes a while to work out what's going on. You could easily imagine you are in a fin de millennium version of Gigi: here a man, his niece and two of her attractive friends finish lunch; off to the side an older man with a beautiful young woman drink white wine, laughing. You hope she isn't his niece. An older couple look sweet and concerned for each other. Everybody comes to Valeries. All the time stunning cakes and patisseries are delivered left and right. It seems safe to predict that in far off years to come people will look into eyes gone pale and say 'Remember that day at Valeries?' In 1996, Patisserie Valerie's seventieth year, they are opening in Regent Street near Piccadilly Circus in May. There are nice surprises planned for there.

V&A MILBURN'S RESTAURANT

Cromwell Road, SW7.   0171 581 2159

Mon noon-5pm   Tues to Sun 10am-5pm

In the Henry Cole wing of the V&A Museum is a vast hangar-like space of elegantly arched natural and cream-painted brickwork and stone-flagged floors, filled with an ample number of pale pine wood benches, tables and chairs, seating at least two hundred people – spaciously – at any one time. A number of circular self service bars stand in the central area of the wing, each one displaying various items from the extensive menu to pick and choose from, allowing a constant flow of customers to glide through to the cash desk without an interminable pile up. At one bar desserts, wine and cheese beckon, while at another, afternoon teas and sandwiches vie for your attention. Regulars who, more often than not, are friends of the V&A, will generally plump for the hot menu of the day and enjoy their 20% discount, or neatly bypass the food queues and seek out the coffee cart which stands alone in an aisle, all the better to serve the espresso drinkers who can enjoy a good coffee at any time of day. In summertime, the restaurant is able to take full advantage of its surroundings by serving sandwiches, salads and strawberries and cream in the exquisite Pirelli Gardens – the ideal spot for a quintessentially English tea. In fact the V&A attracts not only millions of people to its exhibitions every year, but also many visitors who come solely for the restful and relaxing atmosphere of the café where daily papers, good food and good coffee can always be found right next door to the country's most astonishing National Treasures.

KING'S ROAD CAFE AT HABITAT

206 King's Road, SW3. 0171 351 1211

10am-5.30pm every day

With it being all too easy to bump into so many eternally bleak pictures of the world today, this discovery will flip the coin on the instant, inviting you to wallow in all that the inhabitants of (and visitors to) London most deserve: a large, airy room flooded with natural light, where expansive wooden tables share the space with ceiling high foliage in vast terracotta pots, both of which highlight the Mediterranean tones of the walls and the beautifully hand painted Italian china. Here, it is virtually impossible not to dream of sun, sand and sea as the hint of music in the background transports you across the Channel, and the generous cappuccino convinces you, even more, that you are already in sunnier climes... Along with a short, varied menu including a hot dish such as char-grilled breast of turkey, new potatoes and herbs, and lighter snacks of ciabatta sandwiches, bagels, and very good cakes and viennoiseries, this café also serves wine with food throughout the day, so encouraging long, languorous lunches, followed by the absolute necessity: a siesta. P.S. This is one of four cafés run by the charming Mr Almodeo.

The original 'Coffee Gallery' in Museum Street is a small sunny spot where the same excellent coffee, fresh, imaginative food and strikingly attractive Italian China are sought after by every local publisher and bookseller in Bloomsbury. The NW3 Café and Tottenham Court Road Café, both at Habitat, enjoy the same popularity, making you long for Mr Almodeo to open up on the corner of every street in London.

CITY HARVEST

38 Buckingham Palace Road, SW1.   0171 630 9781

Mon to Fri 7am-5pm   Sat & Sun 8am-4pm

If you get in the neighbourhood of the Palace don't miss City Harvest. The owner sleeps only sporadically, we are told by his admiring neighbours. The reason being that he wakes up thinking of new surprises for his multitude of happy customers. Whether you need fortification before, or after the garden party, or strength to make sure you are able to rise after being knighted, (not being able to get up for Her Majesty... well it doesn't bear thinking about) this is the place. The coffee doesn't come much better. The choice of good food is excellent. There is a line outside here every day for things to take away. There is even a 'surprise dish' and no record of anybody not wanting another surprise. Hughie, a neighbour so well known that he gets letters from all over the world addressed simply 'Hughie Buckingham Road', says that Miguel is the kindest man in London, and to say that 'The food is amazing'. So, we told you.

FRESCO
24 Broadway, Westminster SW1   0171 222 2129
Mon to Fri 6am-8pm   Sat & Sun 8am-4pm
After you've seen where your government sits and your poets lie, and sorted out which were which, you may want to put your own feet up, get some coffee and rest a bit. Help is Nigh. Proceed directly across the road from Westminster Abbey the few yards along Tothill Street to Broadway where you will find Fresco immediately on your left. Here is a traditional Italian café with good coffee and good food. There's lots of fresh basil and olive oil around and dishes with sun dried tomatoes and aubergines as well as mozarella, Parma ham and seafood. Good sandwiches ready to go are made here each morning. Light or serious food is available from six in the morning until dusk. Fresco will set up a picnic if you are going to St James Park, or prepare food for pretty well anything you can think of. On the way down Tothill Street you will have noticed a small version of Fresco. If it isn't humming with customers you may not make it to Broadway, the people here will look after you just as well as around the corner. Fresco is essential if you are going to the passport office or New Scotland Yard and is not far from Buckingham Palace.

HAMLET COFFEE SHOP
12 Artillery Row, SW1.   0171 828 9040
Mon to Fri 7am-5pm   Sat & Sun 10am-3pm
If the coffee here makes you ready to take on any challenge, you couldn't be in better hands: this is the only café in London we came upon that makes provisions not only for regulars looking for a good place to hang out, but also for those looking for some fun in the way of Bungee Jumping. If on the other hand you just want to loiter and read a paper over good coffee, that's all right too, and Sam and Hamlet will give you some breakfast, a toasted ciabatta with tomato and mozarella or any other great sandwich from a long long list – or some excellent homemade soup. This place has quickly accumulated a large local following and you'll understand why.

THE WELL

2 Eccleston Place, SW1. (entrance in Elizabeth Street) 0171 730 7303
9.30am-6pm every day

If you are suffering from wanderlust (due to lack of sun and fun?) and
your departure point is Victoria Station, you have every chance of
setting off on the right foot with a stopover at The Well. More than just
a watering hole, run in conjunction with St. Michael's Church, this café
offers a naturally calm contrast to the chaos and mundanities of the
station 'kiosks'. On entering, you are greeted by the greatest pleasure –
the scent of freshly roasted coffee lingering on the air, (more often than
not the Paris blend used for espresso and cappuccino) which reminds
you, as you sample it, to slip a bag into your luggage on leaving, as it is
sold by weight at one end of the café and is probably the best value
coffee around. Trusting you have time enough to stay a little longer, any
one of the freshly prepared dishes will set you up for your journey, (one
at least always being vegetarian) with the noticeably handmade cakes,
scones and biscuits more than reminding you of what you are about to
leave behind. (Or about to come back to.) That said, we can assure you
that the friendly helpers, great coffee and good food will still be here to
greet you on your return, reassuring you that the good things in life so
often remain where you left them.

THE GRAND CAFE

11 South Molton Street W1. 0171 629 0549
Mon to Sat 7.30am-5.45pm   later in Summer

Halfway down South Molton Street there is a café which has one of the
most authentic Italian pedigrees in London. Its owner Mr. Giacometti is
a nephew of the brothers who made so many people happy for so long in
their magnificent Soho restaurant, Hostaria Romana on Dean Street. Not
wanting to run a full scale restaurant himself, Mireno has instead made
the Grand Café into a busy vibrant place where you can drop in and have
coffee and light food at any time of the day. It is often as busy at five
o'clock as at lunchtime. Although Mireno dismisses the suggestion that
he does anything special, and asserts that he just does what he grew up
learning to do to make customers happy, his face comes alive as he
discusses the café and his customers. You can sit outside, or in, and after
you've been to The Grand Café you won't be sorry you took the trouble
to walk the few extra steps to the middle of this street.

LA MADELEINE PATISSERIE AND CAFE

5 Vigo Street, W1.   0171 734 8353

Mon to Sat 8am-7pm

After a hard day's shopping along Regent Street or Savile Row this is the place to revive yourself. With an overwhelming sense of having walked straight into a popular café in the 8th arrondissement of Paris, as the regulars from across the road at Air France discuss the threat of yet more strike action whilst nibbling on their Croques Monsieurs, and the men from the French Consulate tuck into the 'plat du jour', (washing it down nicely with a bottle or two of Pouilly Fumé), you could not do better than take the weight off your feet, order an espresso 'simple mais bien fort', and let your mind drift off to the Boulevard Saint Michel and its sister cafés. Decor is stylish and refreshingly simple with well spaced marble topped tables and delightful prints on the walls. A perfect place to rendezvous as testified to by the many regulars and patrons from as far afield as Japan who enjoy anything from Les Snacks such as Salade Nicoise to Grilled Salmon Steak with Béarnaise Sauce. The great variety of pastries is quite superb. Classico beans ensure excellent coffee. Alcohol with food only.

CAFE DE COLOMBIA

The Museum of Mankind,

6 Burlington Gardens, W1. 0171 287 8148

Mon to Sat 10am-4.30pm   Sun 2.30pm-5pm

Paradise for the coffee lover! A marvellous venue sponsored by the Colombian Coffee Federation, just off Regent and Bond Streets. Perhaps, before savouring the delights of this establishment you may wish to view the totally fascinating and ever changing exhibitions illustrating the variety of Non-Western societies and cultures. The atmosphere within the café is relaxed and soothing with a pleasant decor that includes generously spaced tables, comfy chairs and marble and wooden flooring. The staff contribute enormously to this ambiance, proving to be both diligent and keen. The coffee is superb and a wide selection is on offer including cappuccino, espresso, filter, latte and iced. Food is of a similar standard and includes soups, salads and sandwich specials all freshly prepared on site. To illustrate its enthusiastic coffee credentials, Café de Colombia does not serve tea!

FORTNUM AND MASON

181 Piccadilly W1. 0171 734 8040

Mon to Sat 9.30am-6pm (Fountain Café 9.30am-11pm)

Fortnum, one of Queen Anne's footmen who ran a used candle business on the side, teamed up with his landlord to set up a grocery shop. Nearly three hundred years later Fortnum and Mason is an undisputed empire of quality, and essential for those in search of fine coffee and more.

There are three places to try coffee: The Fountain offers cappuccino, espresso or cafetières of smooth Colombian or Brazilian coffee, you can also try excellent speciality coffees – one from the slopes of the Poas Volcano in Costa Rica, or beans from San Augustin in the Andes. In the morning you might find regulars checking the state of their assets in the Financial Times, simultaneously eulogising a new polish for cherrywood furniture as they sip. To maintain your cover, focus on the murals showing the misters Fortnum and Mason on their quests for 'superior' coffee, cocoa, tea and sugar across the continents.

Indecision is rife here, the menu is an A to Z of treats: sundaes, sodas, sorbets, salads, sandwiches, scones and shortbread. Ask for a pastry and you will be presented with a tray of them just baked a few floors up; sticky and laden with apricots, pears, prunes or raisins. Service is unhurried and professional without the frostiness or brusqueness that some establishments feel is fashionable.

On the fourth floor, the St James is a more stately affair where you can have a tranquil morning coffee surrounded by evocative canvases of racing tea clippers and schooners on the high seas. There is also the possibility of Cumberland sausage, Loch Fyne kippers, wild mushrooms and English muffins. Here in the afternoon you will find a busy but civilised tea in process often accompanied by light piano music.

If this sounds like a daunting visit to Lady Windermere, head downstairs to The Patio, a more relaxed and airier restaurant where you can have what you want when you want it, from 9.30am to 5.30pm. The Patio looks over the food hall below. It is here that the various worlds that Fortnum and Mason serve so expertly, really meet. Old customers with hats and gloves sit close by tourists in sneakers. Neither will be disappointed.

EMPORIUM COFFEE BAR
42 James Street, W1. 0171 224 1493
8am-midnight every day
A strikingly simple insignia and happy people chatting over cappuccinos on the terrace invite you into this fresh new café, where aquamarine paintwork and delicate pinewood and metal furniture encourage you to sit and linger awhile. If you can resist the amazing homemade cakes that greet you on arrival, then settle for a great coffee made from an immaculately maintained machine, and browse over the light Continental menu, or the choice of European cheese and charcuterie platters served with appropriate wine. (Alcohol is licensed here without having to order food.) This café has been designed for versatility so if you arrive on a Saturday morning, the brightly lit interior will be bustling with families tucking into croissants, (bread and viennoiseries are delivered fresh daily) whereas a few hours later the subtle mellow lighting and gentle music will prompt you to relax and unwind at the bar whilst catching up on the day with the friendly staff.

CAFE LIBRE
22 Great Marlborough Street, W1. 0171 437 4106
Mon to Sat 7.30am-midnight   Sun 9.30am-10pm
Ideally located in the heart of London's West End, next to the Palladium Theatre, opposite Carnaby Street, the Café Libre is perfectly situated for tourists, shoppers and theatre goers alike. You will be welcomed by courteous staff of every nationality and once inside will be captivated by the lively café bar atmosphere created by a clever blend of decor, music and lighting. Food is served throughout the day from 7.30am: breakfast is till midday, then a wide selection of continental and English dishes take over catering for all tastes including many for vegetarians. One thing is for certain; the mouthwatering display of French patisseries means you cannot leave without trying at least one of them, though they all taste even better when accompanied by a great coffee from the list including cacaoccino, iced

and many more. Reasonably priced and with no minimum charge, Café Libre attracts a large following of loyal regulars who come from far and wide to seek out this happy atmosphere for a relaxing break.

CAFFE NERO

225 Regent Street, W1.   0171 491 8899
Mon to Sat 7.30am-7pm   Thurs till 8pm   Sun 10am-6pm

Though there was nothing remotely like Nero around here, four days after this café opened in the second week of March it seemed as though the place had been there for years. Their professionalism seems to allow Caffè Nero to put down just about anywhere within sniffing range of folk whose 'good coffee sensors' will lead them to the well, so the place was instantly buzzing. High round tables and counters topped with Rojo Alicante marble make the café warm and welcoming. Chrome chairs with black wicker seats maintain the hard edge Nero feel. The usual great coffee you expect from Caffè Nero is expertly and quickly produced in full view, which is more important than you might think, and all you have to do is decide which good pastries you want, relax and sip. The spark and imagination of the people here make sure that Nero, a winner, keeps on winning.

CAFE WHITTARD

43 Carnaby Street, W1. 0171 437 1107
Mon to Sat 10am-6pm

Carnaby Street is not what it used to be. The centre for peace, love and flower power that was swinging so wildly thirty years ago, has been gracefully transforming itself back in time over the past few years to its classical facades of Georgian London wherein, not surprisingly, a huge range of 'new' shops are displaying their wares. One such merchant so appropriate to this bygone era is Whittard. Specialising in fine teas and coffees on a grand scale, they entice their customers in with lively window displays of gifts, china, gadgets, machines and accessories covering all areas of tea and coffee. As you browse, your senses come alive and your taste buds dream. In vain?...No! For at the top of the stairs is the prettiest room of natural pine tables specifically set aside for the consumption of treats from downstairs: Santos and Java; Colombian; Kenya Peaberry; Mocha and Mysore; Flowery Orange Pekoe; Jasmin; Lapsang Souchong… poetic names which, on tasting, inspire poetry. And to enhance your tastings, there are the most irresistible homemade cakes and generously filled sandwiches to help your pen to flow (which it surely will), if not on the first visit, then the second, third, fourth...)

CHARTIER

46 Dorset Street, W1. 0171 486 2330
Mon to Fri 7.30am-5pm   Sat 9.30am-5pm

From the South of France, by way of Paris, Francois was so taken with
the atmosphere of the restaurant of this name in Montmartre, that he
decided to use it when he opened his own place. The Andronicas coffee
is really good. With it you can have a croissant, or perhaps a piece of
carrot pineapple and walnut cake, which is for the Gods. Unless of
course the Gods are already munching one of Francois' sandwiches. This
could well be the case, as folk around here believe his sandwiches are the
best in London, and wouldn't hesitate to lay one on any passing God.
Anybody searching for such things shouldn't go around the place
handing out sandwich awards, without first checking the product at
Chartier. The Coronation Chicken sandwich is, indeed, amazing, and
smoked salmon with dill, fromage frais and mustard ain't bad either.
And there are many more. You can enjoy all this while basking in the
true Parisian atmosphere of a mural of Georges Seurat's Sunday in the
Parc by Rosalind Buckland.

PATISSERIE VALERIE

The Royal Institute of British Architects
66 Portland Place, W1. 0171 580 5533
Mon to Sat 8am-6pm (till 9pm for exhibitions & events)

Take a stroll along Portland Place a few minutes walk from Oxford
Circus. You will not be disappointed. Here within a magnificent
building opened by King George V, home to RIBA, you'll find Patisserie
Valerie. Enter through a massive doorway into a hallway, and sweep up
to the first floor via an Art Deco Marble Staircase. Within the café,
magnificent standard lamps of the period line the entire length of one
wall. Windows and doors reach up to the ceiling and provide a light,
spacious interior, and lead onto a popular sun terrace. After visiting one
of the events or Galleries here, take lunch, served all day, that includes
pasta dishes, prawn and smoked salmon salad and of course pastries par
excellence. Delicious coffee is available such as espresso, cappuccino, and
a selection of Mocha, Parfait, and Colombian for cafetières.

PATISSERIE VALERIE AT SAGNE

105 Marylebone High Street, W1. 0171 935 6240
Mon to Fri 8am-7pm   Sat 8am-6pm   Sun 9am-6pm

This famous café with its splendid murals, established in the 20s by
M. Sagne from Verlay in Switzerland who made wonderful chocolate

and patisseries here, has recently been taken over and given a lease of life into the third millennium by Patisserie Valerie. The café has been extended and the famous mural of the South of France matched almost to perfection. The cakes in the window make men behave like small boys excitedly rushing in and out to choose and choose again before ordering. Though so close to Oxford Street this part of Marylebone High Street is a village where everybody knows each other. Some have been coming here since the 1920s. Not all were happy when Sagne got taken over. They are now. Valerie's have kept favourite pastries and cakes like Madeira, almond macaroons and dishes like chicken and mushroom vol au vent, while bringing their own immense array of wonders. The coffee is excellent. So is the tea. Underneath the restaurant there is another vast and busy world with people like Xavier, a great chocolatier from Barcelona, excitedly sculpting Belgian chocolate marvels that astonish the eye. There are enough marzipan animals to make Noah blink: hippos, camels, elephants, cows, frogs, hedgehogs, ladybirds and even penguins. No wonder the people upstairs look soignée.

VILLANDRY DINING ROOMS

89 Marylebone High Street, W1. 0171 224 3799
Mon to Sat 8.30am-6pm (open once a month for dinner)
Here, behind a discreet frontage, lies a magical sanctuary which stands for all that is most heavenly in the world of food... Rosalind Carrarini, a

pastry chef, and her husband Jean-Charles, run this shop which in the first instance is a delicatessen of supreme quality and originality: travelling for two months of the year, they discover treasured products from all over the world, and the result is a kaleidoscope of superb products and such 'retrouvés' as Pâtes de Fruits d'Auvergne, original Panaforte, Calissons d'Aix, Old Cape Farm Stall Jams and Bette's Diner Wild Cranberry Scone mix – not to mention sixty varieties of cheese 'à point', such as Reblochon, Tome de Savoie and Gorgonzola to make you drool over... From early in the morning Villandry opens as a restaurant, serving home made viennoiseries, a sumptuous full breakfast and the vital ingredient: double-roasted pure Colombian coffee, meticulously selected for its quality as with everything here. As lunchtime approaches, Rosalind's cooking comes into its own: desserts feature wonderfully and the menu alone, (which varies every day) gives you an idea of just how imaginative the food will be, for example: double soup of red and yellow peppers with tomato jelly; roast leg of lamb with tomato and cannelloni bean stew; and date, pecan tart with maple crème Anglaise... Villandry opens only once a month for dinner in the evenings. Do book in advance so as to enjoy an unforgettable meal in equally memorable surroundings.

CYBERIA - CYBERCAFE

39 Whitfield Street, W1. 0171 209 0982
Mon to Fri 11am-10pm   Sat & Sun 10am-9pm
I've seen the future: it's here. Welcome to the UK's first public access Internet Café. In an ultra friendly atmosphere you can surf the net and explore the ever changing world of electronic communications. You don't need to know a thing about computers to come here, that's the great thing. Everyone is welcome, from businessmen and students to grannies. If you like, fully trained "Cyberhosts" will guide even the most hardened technophobe into the World of Cyberspace. Of course you can just pop in for a cup of good coffee, a delicious sandwich, relax and read a newspaper. Decor is simple and imaginative with steel grey work-stations, chrome/steel ceiling fan, plenty of computer screens and lots of well spaced tables to sit at. You can also perch at a counter to look out at the street life. It's fun and relaxed, not at all sterile or intimidating. The choice of coffee is excellent and includes espresso, caffè latte, cappuccino and filter. The simple menu includes a great range of freshly made sandwiches, soups, salads and pastries. And it's all served by great staff who really are keen to make sure you come back again!

HEAL'S CAFE

196 Tottenham Court Road, W1.   *0171 580 2522*
Mon to Sat 10am-6pm   Thurs till 7.30pm

Heading up Tottenham Court Road with traffic at a complete standstill (more often than not) and exhausts belching forth carbon monoxide at a terrifying rate, don't forget that there is a perfect escape from all this a mere stone's throw away. With not an ounce of effort, you can be transported to the civilised calm of the Heal's Café on the 1st floor where fresh white table cloths and dark wood chairs are spread across a prettily tiled floor, and at either end of the room padded benches and cushions nestle up to the walls where warm lighting and rich drapes create an impression of intimacy. The coffee is pure Colombian Estate – strong and heartwarming, served in cafetières as well as from a Faema machine, and a cross section of intriguing classical music quietly washes over you as you leaf through up-to-the-minute 'glossies' or read the day's papers. Whatever the hour, the all day menu offers you just what you fancy: home made soup and salad, toasted baguette sandwiches or a selection of biscuits and desserts beautifully and temptingly displayed. From midday, the two course fixed price menu for under ten pounds serves dishes such as home made spicy lentil and tomato soup followed by red onion and fresh herb tart with excellent coffee completing the meal. (If you happen to linger till tea time, cream teas are served from 3pm.) With charming, discreet service and an extensive bar list, (alcohol is licensed throughout the day) this café is somewhere to pass a very pleasing couple of hours – and you certainly shouldn't allow less time than this, as it is far too hard to leave.

MANGES-TU

29 Rathbone Place, W1.   0171 631 0678
Mon to Sat 7.30am-5pm

This excellent French café came about quite naturally: the owners Neil and Ken spent all their spare time in France, Ken in Provence, Neil sailing with his family along the Normandy coast, waking up to the smells and sounds of the ports. So why not bring the food they loved to England, they thought... The baguettes and croissants are from a French bakery. Almost everything else is made on the spot to recipes so good that you wonder how you ever satisfied your taste buds before. Consequently, Manges-Tu has an increasingly large following for the wonderful things to take away: great sandwiches, beautifully packed salads with dressings served separately in tiny containers, homemade pizzas, quiches to put the French to shame, fruit tartelettes, homemade cheesecake, yogurts reminding you of what the French do so well, and not forgetting the vital ingredient – the reason the whole idea came about – great French coffee. If you avoid the lunchtime queues there will certainly be room to sit at the wicker bistro chairs in this sunny room or perch at the counter to watch the passing Charlotte Street life whilst tucking into your casse-croute, sipping your café au lait and keeping in touch with life across the Channel by way of Le Monde, Le Figaro or Paris Match.

AMATO

14 Old Compton Street, W1. 0171 734 5733
Mon to Sat 8am-10pm   Sun 10am-10pm

Every now and then you get totally and delightfully surprised. Arrive late at a new café in Soho to be charmingly greeted by the young manager, led past a completely breathtaking display of pasticceria to the person waiting for you. You needn't have worried, she is happily sipping fresh orange juice as she reads the menu. She is more beautiful than the movie star whose image floats on the wall above her. Some good coffee is brought, and it being a quiet moment in the late afternoon, the manager, Daniel, sits to chat. His enthusiasm is infectious, and as

wonderful things are brought to try, he tells us about the history of coffee shops in Soho, and in seventeenth century London. After a bit, the chef comes and joins us: Ugo is a legend of London. Even to people who have never heard his name. In fact he has meant so much to so many Londoners that the authorities should declare him a National Treasure, and stop him from ever leaving if he should think to do so, which is unlikely. This is because Ugo's second name is Amato, and he owns the place. After many years as the head chef at Patisserie Valerie which for so long has been the most famous coffee shop in London, Ugo has just opened up for business here. His partner is the long time former owner of Valerie. Amazing it is to talk to Ugo. He tells of mouthwatering delicacies that are, and were. And of his dreams of pastries that never were... Those that are here include, Delizia de Cassis aux Pommes (delicate blackcurrant mousse, caramelised apple and crème de cassis liqueur) and wonders with names like Delizia di Mandorla, a Roman specialty, Brazilian (coffee mousse with a whisky liqueur) Giotto (tiramisu topping and chocolate mousse combination) and many more. The time passes blissfully. As you leave you look at Marilyn Monroe who may have just licked her lips.

BAR ITALIA

22 Frith Street, W1. 0171 437 4520
Open 24hrs every day

The illustrious boxing record of the legendary Rocky Marciano, "Undefeated heavyweight champion of the World" hangs in pride of place behind the rattling till at Bar Italia, the champ's gloves dangling alongside. Rocky was a friend of Signor Polledri who opened the Frith Street shop in 1949, the business passing through to his son and now to his grandson, the current owner. The original design has been preserved in a recent refurbishment with inlaid floor, wood panelled walls, and a long bar punctuated by an engine red steaming Gaggia coffee machine and piles of rather functional croissants and pastries. There are two flickering fruit machines at the far end of the room, and a giant TV screen showing MTV or football, groups of coffee drinkers gathered beneath. But it all happens in the mirror at Bar Italia. Sitting on a stool, leaning against the ledge and staring down the length of the reflecting glass; talking heads, coffee cups brandished by gesticulating hands, curling smoke from cigarettes slipped between fingers. And the barmen in the background slicing sandwiches, polishing glasses.

Open 24 hours a day, 7 days a week the atmosphere and social mix changes with the hands on the clock, from early rising Italian businessmen snatching breakfast to late night revellers trying to sober up or boosting adrenalin at 4 am. It is often noisy, with loud music or sport, clattering crockery and an awful lot of chatting and laughter. Bar Italia is definitely one of those places which could tempt you to buy a coffee cup as a souvenir. Like the "Café des Flores" in Paris, this Soho bar basks in the glow of legend, and like its St Germain cousin, has decided to retail its sought-after crockery emblazoned with the inimitable swirling green script. Unfortunately, the prices do reflect the cachet of drinking this particular blend under this particular roof, with a large cappuccino costing 2.60. Unmissable, but be prepared to shell out.

CAFFE NERO
43 Frith Street, W1.   0171 434 3887
8am-2am every day

A modern coffee bar with a purpose…to be the best. A few years ago folk would have said that anybody setting up a place such as this head to head with Bar Italia must be foolhardy, blessed by the Gods, or else think they know something others can't see. Caffè Nero is one of the great meeting places of Soho, buzzing from morning till morning, and not just on the great coffee. A mixture of media, models, young, not so young, fashionable, grungey and, after dark, the exotic, gather here. And if you aren't any of the above and just want to pause, ponder, and peer over your coffee, strategically set on the corner of Frith and Old Compton Streets this is one of the best places in these parts to keep an eye on the passing parade.

CYBERSPY CAFE

15 Golden Square, W1. 0171 287 2242
Mon to Fri 10am-8pm   Sat 10am-6pm

Located in Golden Square this is one of the latest Internet cafés to hit the scene. Keilash, the owner, has created a refreshingly 'user friendly' venue, with a warm welcoming atmosphere, striking decor and a great sense of space. The staff are genuinely friendly and willing to assist you in surfing the highway if you wish. Tuition is also available. There are plenty of full multi-media machines to sit at, or just relax at one of the many spaciously arranged three-legged tables. There are fresh flowers all around and regular high quality art exhibitions on the vast wall space. Food is freshly prepared on the premises with salads and sandwiches made to order. All sandwiches are 'double deckers' using high quality thick cut bread. Jacket potatoes come with an amazing choice of fillings; or perhaps just drink one of the excellent coffees whilst taking in the magazines and newspapers provided. The choice includes cappuccino, espresso, decaf and flavoured coffee.

FIRST OUT

52 St Giles High Street, WC2. (Near Centre Point) 0171 240 8042
Mon to Sat 10am-11pm   Sun noon-10.30pm

Reputed to be the first "out" café in London, this gay venue has certainly established a great reputation as a place to meet friends and relax. Set on two levels, the ground floor has a light, fresh feel to it with plenty of tables, flowers in abundance and a No Smoking policy. Exhibitions including paintings and photography are regularly displayed on the walls. The "Centre of Operations", the kitchen and coffee bar also work from here. Below in the basement a more intimate environment exists, where smokers are given free rein. There's a bar and again plenty of tables. A community noticeboard, fresh flowers and innovative lighting involving lengths of twisted copper tubing, help create a terrific ambiance.

First Out really is "attitude" free and as a consequence a great cross-section of the community use it regularly. About the food: it's an all vegetarian menu, is extremely imaginative and varied and is made fresh on the premises daily. It includes dishes such as spicy peanut curry, soups, a variety of salads, a great selection of filled rolls and bagels – plus yummy cakes. Coffee arrives via an Italian Brasilia machine working to maximum capacity to deliver hundreds of cappuccinos and espressos to regulars awaiting their chosen fix, safe in the knowledge that it's consistently better than good. Filter coffee is also on offer. So – a great place to chill out, either with friends, or indeed, on your own.

FREEDOM BAR

60-66 Wardour Street, W1. 0171 734 0071

11am-3am every day

Freedom, London. A former catering equipment showroom transformed into an award-winning café and bar. An award-winning café and bar transformed into a theatre, a cabaret venue, an exhibition space and, from Autumn '96, the inspiration for a TV show. Despite popular pressure to create Freedom Manchester and Amsterdam, Freedom London remains unique. On the corner of Old Compton and Wardour Streets, it could almost be missed, only the logo discreetly etched onto a large plain window opposite the Las Vegas gambling parlour marks this nondescript building as the place to be, whilst double doors open onto a long room with a bulb-shaped space at the far end. The walls are painted plain white, the floor is polished hard wood. There are grey and white formica tables with black metal chairs, and the ever-changing multicoloured lights of the Las Vegas glitter in through the window, their colours softened by a thin haze of cigarette smoke. Freedom has a real bar in true USA tradition: long, white and chrome, with rows of bottles, glasses and cans of beer. The real bar has a real drinks list: spirits, iced shots, wines, champagne, cocktails, fresh juices, iced teas and health drinks. And the coffee is seriously good: ristretto for the dedicated caffeine addict, iced cappuccino, latte, mocha, and flavoured and alcoholic delights. (The LA hot chocolate with marshmallows and the hot vanilla milk are not to be missed.)

This place is friendly. The staff in black and white Freedom T-shirts give great service, whether you want just coffee, or the delicious all-day, most-of-the-night food: savouries, salads, indulgent puddings and imaginative dips, crackers and salsas for in between. After 11pm, international cabaret acts take to the stage in the downstairs bar, and upstairs mellows down...perfect for coffee at 2am. Perfect anytime.

JAVA JAVA

Rupert Street W1. 0171 734 5821

Mon to Thurs 10am-10pm   Fri 10am-11pm
Sat 11am-11pm   Sun 1pm-8pm

This tiny space has been filled with all manner of good things imaginable, including nine origins and blends of the freshest coffee beans roasted to specification in small quantities and brightly presented and sold under the 'Java Java' name, along with a massive range of all that is sweet smelling in teas, (60 to be more precise) and hot chocolate to make you swoon over. Sitting on cheery red stool-like chairs at marble tables, coffee is served in a multitude of ways, each one seeming curiously better than the last. Along with strong, sweet-smelling espresso and cappuccino, caffè latte is a great favourite here, though caffè brevè is a variation rarely found elsewhere and well worth discovering, with or without one of the flavoured syrups from Seattle. Freshly made sandwiches and luscious homemade cakes more than satisfy your appetite, (they, alone, are worth popping in for) and in summertime these are great accompanied by fresh fruit smoothies – another American dream happily reaching the city. With lively music and a good selection of papers and magazines to read over the hum of nearby chatter, this friendly haunt can easily turn what was to be a five minute coffee stop into an hour of pleasure. (And don't forget to sign the mirror before leaving.)

MAISON BERTAUX

28 Greek Street, W1. 0171 437 6007
9am-8pm every day
Established in 1871, Maison Bertaux is a fabled pillar of Soho society, celebrated for its eccentric blend of bohemian hospitality, sublime croissants and decadent patisseries. The original shop and bakery nestles at the Shaftesbury Avenue end of Greek Street, a neighbour to that renowned watering hole, The Coach and Horses. 'La Patronne' is the actress, Michelle Wade. She darts and hovers like a dazzling dragonfly around the shop and kitchen, alternately chastising, teasing and chatting with staff and customers alike. Choose to take refreshment downstairs, and see the trays of freshly baked croissants, gateaux and savouries carried past by the (often gorgeous) chefs. Take a rest in the upstairs tea room, and be either charmed or exasperated by the sometimes erratic service from Miss Wade's international minestrone of staff, or by the opinions or subject matter of the eclectic clientèle's conversation. Then try and imagine this crowded convivial room as a critically acclaimed theatre, for that is exactly its transformation whenever the Maison Bertaux Theatre Club chooses to mount a production. The scent of baking and fresh coffee is merely an appetizer for the main event. The food here tastes delicious, and the café au lait is hot and frothy, made with a blend from the local Algerian Coffee Stores. At this café institution everyone seems to have a favoured indulgence with some customers even christened by their regular order: 'Almond Slice! How lovely to see you!'. By popular vote, the French almond croissants, cheese and ham croissants, lunchtime savouries, tarte au citron and strawberry tarts are unmissable. And when romance blossoms into wedlock, a chef can be seen staggering out of the door balancing a towering croquenbouche before him. Truly a landmark on any café society map.

OLD COMPTON CAFE

34 Old Compton Street, W1.   0171 439 3309

Open 24 hours

For many people in the heart of Soho, this is their only port of call for refreshment. Enter a café that is run by really friendly staff and has a buzzing, cosmopolitan atmosphere any time of the day or night. There are lots of tables to sit at inside, or you can watch the world go by under canopy or at chrome chairs and tables fronting the establishment. Decor is simple and effective with spot-lights covering ceiling and walls clad in burnished metal, while above is painted a glorious deep blue, interspersed with thin-tapered strips of mirrors.

The food counter displays a mouthwatering selection of delights, all freshly made on the premises. Sandwiches, made to order, include grilled chicken and roast vegetables. There are many "Compton Café Specials" including vegetarian salads and full fry-up breakfasts. Fruit salads are delicious. The café produces its own special blend of freshly roasted coffee, ground on the premises. It is enthusiastically served to a high standard and includes espresso, cappuccino, caffè latte, mocha, filter and decaffeinated.

PATISSERIE VALERIE

44 Old Compton Street, W1. 0171 437 3466

Mon to Fri 8am-8pm   Sat 8am-7pm   Sun 10am-6pm

On hearing of this book, the first words off almost everybody's lips have been 'Valerie's in Soho'.

It would be hard to find a soul who has been part of anything interesting in London who hasn't been to this place. So much so, that the owners have had to open outposts in strange places as far afield as Marylebone and Knightsbridge to save Soho from being completely

swamped by pilgrims. In the sixties, when Soho was still Soho but being 'discovered' (just like Africa and America, the locals were getting on with life, and didn't know they were lost) Valerie's was the meeting point.

The management made the 'discoverers' leave their photographers outside so local citizens could carry on their lives undisturbed (discovery being abhorrent to many of them). Indeed some of the inmates were extremely wide, such as film producers and distributors, or even record producers who hadn't found it necessary to confuse their artists with news of such things as publishing rights. Others were just ordinary gangsters, politicians, and what are now quaintly known as sex workers. Tables were shared, and sometimes people entering together had to sit apart, or even at different tables, making conversations sometimes confused, or disjointed.

So much so, that it had been known for a person who had merely come to have some of the wonderful pastries on offer with a decent cup of coffee, while trading a little jewellery, to leave as a real skuldugger and find himself doing a few years behind a desk as a record producer. Valerie's has gone from strength to strength and with its wonderful patisseries and coffee deserves to. There are now branches in Covent Garden, Knightsbridge, Marylebone and Portland Place, with Regent Street opening in May.

THE STAR CAFE & BAR

22b Great Chapel Street W1.   0171 437 8778
Mon to Sat 7am-6.30pm
This unique café, a visual feast and a delight for the tastebuds, is wonderfully preserved by Mario, whose father, Ambrogio from the Gulf of Salerno, started it in 1934. Ambrogio worked at an earlier Star which came about because the owner took the advice of The Star's racing tipster during a lucky streak. Ambrogio brought the name here and the luck seems to have come too. The Star is warm, bright, cheerful. There's a treasure trove here from a bygone era. The Bovril, Will's Gold Flake Cigarettes, and Ogden's Famous Walnut Plug posters are a delight. There are unusual metal signs, ancient cigarette and peanut dispensers, old radiograms, cash tills and giant thermometers. Stylish ceiling lamps, swirling fans, flowers on the tables and lots of green foliage add charming touches. The café is on two floors, upstairs there are lots of windows, so it's wonderfully light. A spiral staircase leads to a delightful intimate dining place, known as The Long Room, once a cellar. There's a terrific wartime feel down here with Churchill posters: Let's Go Forward Together, and Women of Britain – Come into the Factories.
All rousing stuff. The food, all freshly prepared here, is good and excellent value. The menu includes delicious thick-cut sandwiches made to order, soups, hamburgers, pasta dishes and salads such as Caesar Salad with breast of chicken. Bangers and Mash are very popular, as are jacket potatoes; you just help yourself to the salad. The good coffee here, ground fresh, includes espresso, cappuccino, latte, mocha, decaffeinated and filter. Newspapers are provided.

THE YARD

57 Rupert Street, W1 (just off Wardour St). 0171 437 2652
Mon to Sat noon-11pm   Sun noon-10.30pm

Located within a courtyard setting complete with cherub fountain, this mixed/gay venue truly is an oasis in the heart of Soho. During the day it offers you a haven from the hustle and bustle of city life, with a great continental café atmosphere, whilst in the evening, being fully licensed, it transforms itself into a much "buzzier" cosmopolitan style bar.

The decor is modern and stylish with fresh flowers abounding on the spaciously arranged tables. The courtyard contributes further to the wonderful ambiance. Here you can sit out and relax, enjoying the terracotta tubs and all they contain, hopefully taking in the sunshine. The warm, welcoming atmosphere is in no small measure due to the staff who are always genuinely helpful. They'll advise you on the deliciously simple menu served until 5pm. Vegetarians as well as carnivores are catered for. Daily specials are on offer plus such delights as Caesar Salad with Quails Eggs, Vegetarian Club Sandwich and Braised Beef and Wild Mushroom Pie.

Own blend coffee is something to look forward to: cappuccinos, espressos, decaf and filtered are available as well as specialities such as French, Jamaican, Irish and Mexican. Or, perhaps try the bottomless cup and have as many top-ups as you like!

THE APOGEE COFFEE HOUSE

3 Leicester Place, WC2. 0171 437 4556
Mon to Thurs & Sun 8am-2am   Fri & Sat 8am-4am

Surrounded by beautiful natural wood and drinking great coffee gives you the feeling that somehow this really is all you need in life. I must add though that mellow lighting, wonderful wall hangings and fresh colourful food does help... and at Apogée all this is for real: the coffee is 100% Colombian, chosen by a true Italian: it is strong, rich and serré – unbeatable, unless you prefer any other way of serving this roast to make you happy (and they will all make you so). Many regulars are discovering this haven which serves delicious fresh food almost 24 hours a day with alcohol licensed with food. The breakfast menu ranges from a quick 'continental' to a full breakfast or healthy muesli. This is served to midday. Soups, salads and Greek dishes then appear, and are not only wonderful, but as with everything here are also amazingly cheap. There are specials of the day to make you chuckle at such as 'Mozaique du village'– keep guessing! Anyway, whatever your hours, your needs and your moods, if you want them, the good things in life are here.

RENDEZ-VOUS CAFE

Leicester Square, WC2. 0171 925 1082

Mon to Thurs 9am-midnight   Fri, Sat & Sun 9am-3am

This prime site, American-sized coffee shop was revamped at the same time as Leicester Square, and can now boast a bright and bustling larger-than-life art deco style interior seating over 100 people at any one time, at brand new polished granite tables with stylish chrome chairs. There is ample room in which to perch at various bars around the place, and a chance to watch the world go by when the tables spread out over a large expanse of the Square, ensuring you a bird's eye view till nearly dawn. With this being their only franchise in the U.K, Java Coast, a Dallas company, import 16 different roasts and blends of coffee here, such as Guatemala Antigua (spicy, smokey and medium) and Sumatra (syrupy Arabica). Many flavoured syrups are on offer too, making the choice of coffee, and the way in which it can be served, infinite... Encountering, as you enter, over 100 varieties of top quality gateaux, (soon to be baked on the premises) cast your eyes over the laden counters, starting with a feast of 16 flavours of ice cream and frozen yogurt, to 14 varieties of cheesecake, and on to multiple choices of cakes, pastries and breads, before reaching the savoury section of bagels, baguettes, pasties...there is too much to take in on your first visit, but once you know your way around, choosing will become a piece of cake.

CAFFE NERO

29 Southampton Street, WC2.   0171 240 3433

Mon to Fri 7am-8pm   Sat 8am-8pm   Sun 9am-7pm

At this outpost of the Caffè Nero Empire marble-topped tables surround the room, where you can perch at black and chrome chairs while black and white lights give the shop an interesting feel. The usual excellent coffee and delectable authentic Italian cakes such as Tarte di mele, plus panini and divine coffee have won this particular coffee shop all the accolades possible in London...this is no surprise. For if you are lucky enough to run into Ian Semp the owner who is one of the most dynamic and restless world travellers, or Antonio who manages Caffè Nero they will pepper the conversation with ideas on whatever subject comes up. They have plenty of these for coffee drinking London so look out for the striking Nero canopies to proliferate.

CAFE PASTA

184 Shaftesbury Avenue, WC2. 0171 379 0198

Mon to Sat 9.30am-11.30pm (till 11pm Sun)

Perfectly situated for theatre goers and Covent Garden shoppers, this is Café Pasta's original flagship restaurant. Now extended into the basement, though remaining the smallest of the six branches, it none the less retains its great pioneering spirit of eight years ago, when the novelty of their wonderful pasta dishes freshly cooked before your eyes took hold of London's imagination right here.

   And as with all great innovators, the ideas keep coming thick and fast. Not only serving their fresh, varied menu (with specials such as egg linguine with garlic, chilli and sun-dried tomatoes, and the endlessly magical Marine Ices chalked on the board daily) Café Pasta now opens from 9.30am right through to the end of the evening, to serve the most generous coffee and viennoiseries to be found in London. In fact, I defy you to resist the basket of treats that tantalise you as you vainly insist on 'Just a strong double espresso please', to start the day: warm croissants oozing chocolate must surely win you over in the end. And to tempt you further, Café Pasta has a ridiculously good offer on a coffee and croissant. Then again if you're stopping for tea, you should linger on for a generous aperitif from the extensive wine list before enjoying the other offers that will by now have reached your ears...

   As always the staff are charming, friendly and very happy to help, making Café Pasta an unfailingly happy place to be. There are high chairs and colouring sheets for children.

MONI'S

42 Monmouth Street WC2.   0171 497 0594

Mon to Sat 9am-11.30pm

Sipping a satisfyingly strong espresso and feeling peckish, on discovering Moni's food you discover enlightenment. For here, in his small naturally furnished café is the most heavenly food you can imagine: imported directly from Lebanon and Cyprus, Moni's food is entirely water-fed organic and free range. In particular, all dishes are of entirely Lebanese origin, such as homous (as you've never tasted before) and Lebanese bread. This is not pitta. Barbecues cooked on an open fire grill before your eyes, (these are not kebabs) and the original Lebanese falafel, tahine and kebbe leave you stunned by the wonder of Moni's real food...his simple philosophy is 'marriage of food': the body fed and nurtured correctly will remain healthy and happy throughout life. Eat here and you will understand this. The excellent coffee and patisseries are served to enhance this philosophy! P.S. 'Coming to a café near you' as Moni is starting to supply other people with his delights.

M.J. BRADLEYS

9 King Street, Covent Garden WC2. 0171 240 5178

Mon to Fri 8am-8.30pm   Sat & Sun 11.30am-8pm

Just around the corner from the world famous Piazza, the Royal Opera House and St. Paul's (the actors' church) designed by Inigo Jones, you'll find this irresistible establishment. Ambiance leans towards the Mediterranean with a refreshingly simple and yet invigorating decor. Plaster 'washed' walls are adorned by exquisite light fittings, and the theme carries on throughout with lamps made from heavy black metal in intricate patterns, the illumination shining through. Furniture, either in the basement or at ground level, is comfortable and substantial, made from solid wood and fine wrought iron. A pretty view of the gardens of Saint Paul's Church adds the finishing touches, and in warm weather you can sit out among the flowers. Food is displayed to perfection and is quite superb. It is all totally fresh and made on the premises. Sandwiches and salads are a particular speciality. Breads include cheese and onion, honey seed, granary and walnut. Choose from an awesome range of fillings or design your own. A good example might be smoked mackerel, spinach and pear in a lemon dressing on carrot bread. Salads are equally imaginative. Staff are delightfully friendly, all the better to serve you the excellent coffee specially roasted for the premises, espresso being served in a clear glass tumbler. Or perhaps just sit outside at a table, read a paper provided and watch the world of Covent Garden go by.

CAFE VALERIE,
8 Russell Street, WC2. 0171 240 0064
Mon to Sat 7.30am–11pm   Sun 9am-6pm
A cultural, historical and gastronomic delight awaits you here in the heart of Covent Garden. Café Valerie, formally Boswells Coffee House, opened as a Tea House in 1752. It played host to London's literati and it is here in 1763 that Mr Boswell, the well-known diarist, met the famous Dr Johnson whose fascinating biography he went on to write.

Today too it is a charming, stylish meeting place. Looking through the latticed windows and seeing the world-renowned delicacies, one can't help but be tempted to walk in. Here you'll find a warm welcoming atmosphere and be attended by loyal enthusiastic staff, some of whom have been working here for many years. Spacious tables, Italian bar-stools and marble counters are the order of the day, set off by exquisite tiled-mirrored walls. Newspapers are provided.

A superb menu covers excellent breakfasts and club sandwiches, fresh pasta, homemade vegetarian quiches and a variety of salads. Words cannot do justice to the quite extraordinary pastries. George, the manager, ensures that the Italian style coffee is served to the highest standards, whether to drink in or take away. The range includes espresso, cappuccino, cafetière, decaf, mocha Italia and iced.

CAFE IN THE CRYPT
St Martin in The Fields Church, WC2.   0171 930 1862
Mon to Sat 10am-8pm
This warm, womb like church crypt has been beautifully and sensitively converted to house both a café and a restaurant. A buffet style restaurant serves a three-course menu at the rear of the crypt, and the Café counter serves an excellent Drury Coffee Mocha-D'Or any way you choose, plus a striking selection of home made sandwiches, cakes and pastries from the middle of the room. Sitting wherever you choose, whether dining, snacking or just drinking good coffee, a warm hum always fills this ancient tombstoned and flagstoned church floor. If you want to be seen, sit between the magnificent brickwork arches; or tuck yourself in beside them if you want to hide away and read a paper. Either way the soft lighting, and gentle classical music playing in the background, enhance this peaceful and soul-soothing coffee stop. The church sells cards and gifts, and visitors form an enthusiastic queue to make brass rubbings.

SEATTLE COFFEE COMPANY

51-54 Long Acre, WC2.   0171 836 2100
Mon to Thur 7am-8pm   Fri 7am-9pm
Sat 10am-9pm   Sun 10am-7pm

The phenomenon of the Seattle coffee movement has arrived in London, and you can now savour the delights right in the heart of Covent Garden. There's a whole new coffee-speak for those in the know, and it can be put to good effect when ordering favourite coffee creations such as Double Tall Skinny Latte or Single Shot No Fun Mocha. The ambiance is tremendously warm and welcoming with the staff exceptionally friendly and helpful and armed with an excellent knowledge of the coffee they serve. The interior is beautifully modern with cheerful lighting, great ambient music and, along the length of one wall, stylishly comfortable bar stools. Coffee really is superb and is specially roasted using the highest quality arabica beans. The choice and style is vast and includes Guatemala, Antigua, Java, Sumatra Lintang and Decaf Colombian. All the drinks can be added to with an extra shot of coffee if you wish, or perhaps a flavoured syrup, like Cherry Mocha, or toasted Marshmallow. The bean blends are available to take away in 8oz valve bags. Newspapers are provided so you can sip, savour and watch the world go by.

Branches opening soon:
25 Kensington High Street, W8. 3 Grosvenor Street, W1.
14 James Street, W1. Waterstones, Cambridge and Edinburgh.

KONDITOR AND COOK AT THE YOUNG VIC THEATRE

66 The Cut, SE1. (Nr Waterloo Station) 0171 620 2700

Mon to Fri 8.30am-11pm   Sat 10.30am-11pm

This stylish café with it's imaginative, clean and fresh decor ensures it is a venue not just popular with theatre goers, but with the local community too. There is a great sense of space here, with an intelligent use of lighting and table arrangements. A large window runs virtually the full length of the establishment, where you can perch yourself upon stools, watching the world go by. Food is quite simply delicious and all freshly prepared on the premises or at the renowned bakery, Konditor and Cook, just around the corner. It is here that head baker, Gerhard Jenne, makes pastries to die for, including superb strudels. The menu also includes mozzarella and tomato salads, fried free-range eggs with award winning Ayrshire bacon, through to soups and specials and "Konditor Sandwiches" built up on hand-baked focaccia. Breakfasts too are a speciality, including fresh baked Normandy butter croissants, and Scottish smoked salmon on toasted organic wholemeal bread. All the staff take pride in the service they provide and offer a great welcome, whether you are popping in just for coffee, or something a little more substantial. About the coffee, it's delicious. A fine range of Brazilian roast, freshly ground on the premises that includes espresso, cappuccino, decaffeinated and iced. And it's all just a stone's throw away from Waterloo.

BRAMAH TEA AND COFFEE MUSEUM

The Clove Building, Maguire Street, Butler's Wharf, SE1

0171 378 0222

10am-6pm every day

If you like, or have an interest in coffee, then you really must pay a visit to this totally absorbing establishment. You'll find it in the heart of the old tea and coffee trade at Butler's Wharf where many of the magnificent old warehouses are still standing. Edward Bramah established the museum in 1992, and is an acknowledged world authority on the tea and coffee trade, having been a tea taster, owner of tea and coffee companies and also author of several books on the subject. This is the world's only complete collection devoted to tea and coffee-making history. It is quite exquisite and includes a glittering array of pictures, ceramics and silver. History and tradition are explored from the 17th Century up to the present day. The tea and coffee room is amazing. Here you can relax in a pool of tranquillity, a calming respite from the rigours of the city. The staff are charmingly helpful and you are very welcome to take refreshment without feeling obliged to see the delights of the Museum. The tables are spaciously arranged within an imaginative setting, surrounded by magnificent artifacts including satirical prints, antique coffee sets, tea-urns and teapots.

Here, quite superb pre-teabag leaf-tea is served including Bramah's own speciality blend. The ground Kenyan Coffee is also excellent and is an exclusive blend. It's all served with great enthusiasm in fine bone-china cups, emblazoned with the Bramah insignia. Adjacent to this, a shop sells a spectrum of related products including ground coffee, slow-infusing orthodox teas, postcards, posters, caddies, books, teapots and coffee makers.

LEITH'S AT THE DESIGN MUSEUM
Shad Thames, SE1. 0171 357 8992
Mon to Fri 11.30am-5.30pm   Sat & Sun noon-5.30pm
A stunning location on the banks of the River Thames with glorious views of Tower Bridge and the surrounding Butler's Wharf Conservation Area. The whole area is a treat, steeped in history and well worth exploring. The Design Museum itself houses two galleries and a lecture theatre and plays host to classic design and state of the art innovations from around the world. There's also a "funky" design shop selling designer led products from key-rings, corkscrews to clocks and coffee pots. Definitely worth a look. Or just relax in the café next to the shop on the ground floor, helped by keen staff, eager to make your visit a pleasure. Just one of the reasons why they're building up a loyal following from regulars in the area. The layout is spacious with highly polished marble floors and massive sliding windows looking out onto the river. During the summer these are open for you to sit outside on a glorious sun terrace. Tables are set well apart with elegant chairs designed by Arne Jacobsen. The café offers a mouth-watering selection of sandwiches – all freshly prepared on a variety of breads. Try anything from poached salmon with tarragon and mayonnaise through to roast beef and horseradish on rye. There are also excellent soups, huntsman pies and terrific cakes. Pride is taken in the Colombian coffee served. Each cup is freshly ground and includes espresso, cappuccino, kaffe Suisse and decaffeinated. If that's not enough, there are flavoured coffees too.

ANDRONICAS
91 Great Eastern Street EC2. 0171 729 4411
Mon to Fri 9am-5.30pm
1993. Holding a wealth of knowledge, quiet commitment and infallible vision, Andrew Knight broke away from the crowd, took roomy premises on the near derelict East side of the City and within three years

is importing, roasting, distributing and serving coffee which is clearly as good as you will find anywhere. From a giant Brazilian Lilla roaster fresh green beans are hot air roasted to an ideal strength according to origin and blend then nitrogen vacuum packed, or ground and packed, to order. (All the roasted beans being sealed within hours.) Discerning choice ensures a consistently high quality of beans. Highly skilled roasters and freshness of the end product mean that through one man, coffee drinkers here now have the opportunity of tasting the sort of coffee previously only dreamed of in far off lands... Here in the East, (the near East) is a beacon, a shrine, a grand hall inviting you in to sit at the marble topped bistro tables or sink into the sofas at the edge of the room with a selection of magazines and daily papers to be glanced at as they wait their turn on the coffee tables in front of you.

To one side, a discreet display of coffee – beans and bags – waits quietly to be bought, (along with a selection of teas) and at the back of the hall, running the length of it, is where the very finest coffee is to be discovered, the majestic Victoria Arduino machine, its spread eagle emblem surveying the scene, magicking the treasure into espresso, cappuccino, caffè latte... every conceivable form of nectar.

All this can be savoured along with an all day menu of the finest sandwiches, patisseries, homemade soups and salads, as daylight spills in through the vast high-silled windows adding to the light of the aisles of moon lamps throwing their own light onto this great hall – once a city bank – now a bank of a very different kind, producing some of the country's most prized treasure.

ASHBY'S

4 Artillery Passage, E1. 0171 247 1830
Mon to Fri 6am-5pm
Located right in the heart of Jack The Ripper territory along a suitably classic Dickensian walkway, interspersed with a fascinating variety of shops. It's also just a few minutes walk away from Spitalfields Market and Brick Lane. A totally fascinating area. Step through the Regency facade into a well lit, intimate Coffee House. It's clean and fresh with a couple of tables, half tiled walls and great old photographs of the East End of London. Newspapers are provided for you to peruse at your leisure. Here you'll be served by friendly, vibrant staff – usually kitted

out in bright, jazzy waistcoats. They'll help you to choose from a truly vast selection of sandwiches all freshly made to order, soups and terrific pasta dishes. The Lavazza coffee is excellent and includes espresso, cappuccino and decaffeinated. It's worth noting that an excellent take-away service is also available – much used by the local community.

CAFE AT THE BETHNAL GREEN MUSEUM OF CHILDHOOD

Cambridge Heath Road, E2. 0181 980 1830

Mon to Thur 11am-4pm   Sat 10am-5pm   Sun 2.30am-5pm

This is an intriguing and fascinating venue and a pretty unusual setting for a café. Originally established in 1872 as part of the V&A museum with the specific aim to "bring National Heritage to the East End of London", it is now a thriving centre highlighting the history of childhood through a variety of exhibitions and various "Themes". At the moment I'm surrounded by all things "Rupert Bear". Bliss! The café is centred on the ground floor and is ideal for families, especially with toddlers and youngsters. All the tables are widely spaced and there's plenty of floor space...ideal for crawling! Games and colouring books are supplied to play with and often there are competitions and a variety of other activities too. The staff of 'Hampton's Catering' are friendly and enthusiastic, serving a wide selection of cold food. Fresh sandwiches on various breads, baguettes and salads with a variety of fillings. A lunch box containing all sorts of goodies is on offer for the kids. Italian cappuccino and espresso are available as is filtered coffee.

FRESCO CAFE BAR

Cabot Square Canary Wharf, E14. 0171 512 9072

Mon to Fri 6am-8pm   Sat & Sun 8am-4pm

The sort of surprise you welcome at a place as new as Canary Wharf, a traditional Italian café, with a wide variety of good food, just like you wished your Moma could have made. The coffee is good. Breakfast is served until noon. These people are serious about providing good service and you can relax here or grab things and run. Fresco has been so successful here that they have taken the space next door, doubling the café's size. Everything has been brought from Modena so they will be even more Italian. Fresco delivers, and given a day's notice they can provide an amazing choice of dishes from their catering menu or pretty well anything you can think up, for a picnic or a banquet.

SEATTLE COFFEE COMPANY

366 Cabot Square East, Canary Wharf, E14. 0171 363 0040
Mon to Fri 7am-7pm   Sat 10am-4pm

Let the Docklands Light Railway whisk you virtually to the front door of this marvellous coffee house. Enter immediately into the fashionable shopping mall, descend an escalator and you're there!

The shop itself is wonderfully stylish and spacious with an imaginative use of bold yellows, blues and reds. There is room to sit and relax at tables or on comfortable bar-stools, where you can almost see your reflection in the highly polished marble surfaces. Display cabinets show off the ever-increasing range of coffee related merchandise, including superb travel mugs, cafetières and coffee grinders. At the centre of the counter-bar is a gorgeous, black Gaggia coffee machine behind which there is a magnificent display of the variety of coffee beans sold. All are superior arabicas from around the coffee regions of the world. The choice is stunning, made to the highest standards, and to the customer's exact specification. The whole concept is that coffee should be fun and that the customer really does come first. The staff are extremely well trained, bright and friendly and will be delighted to advise you in any way they can.

Simple, fresh food is on offer, including bagels, croissants and cookies. Newspapers are on hand. And why not ask about the Coffee Club which can entitle you to a free coffee?

Branches opening soon:

25 Kensington High Street, W8. 3 Grosvenor Street, W1.
14 James Street, W1. Waterstones, Cambridge and Edinburgh.

THE ALMEIDA CAFE-BAR

Almeida Street, Islington, N1. 0171 226 0931
Mon to Sat 10am-11pm

Mention "The Almeida" and many people would perhaps think of a theatre with a first class international reputation, producing "the classics" and innovative new writing: a real power house of dramatic and artistic success. And, of course, they'd be right – but there is more! The café-bar is a delight, especially so during the day when its warm, welcoming atmosphere provides a truly relaxing environment. It's not just theatre-goers using it either. Many people find it an ideal location to meet friends, read a paper or perhaps take some refreshment.

The split-level layout is spacious and yet intimate with plenty of "corners" for those requiring a little privacy. Bleached pine panelling and lovely old wooden floor-boards, coupled with imaginative lighting from theatre "spots" and stylish black and white photos all create a soothing ambiance. Several sky-lights, some with a profusion of foliage, and windows looking out onto the street, also contribute to this effect. From behind the wonderfully long bar, many continental beers and wines are dispensed. It's also where the blackboard menu is displayed. The food is good, simple fare, freshly prepared on the premises with the emphasis towards vegetarian. Choose from homemade soups such as spinach and coconut, a variety of salads and cheeses, vegetarian moussaka and delights such as leek and potato and cauliflower au gratin. Homemade cakes are excellent as are the desserts. The dark Italian roast coffee is always good and freshly ground on the premises – including espresso, cappuccino, filtered and decaffeinated. Finally, it's worth noting that the staff are a friendly, enthusiastic lot. All the more reason to pop into this charming venue, read a paper provided, including "The Stage", and allow the cares of the world to just drift away.

ANGEL CAFE BAR

65, Graham Street, Islington N1. 0171 608 2656
Mon to Sat noon-midnight   Sun noon-11.30pm
Just a few minute's walk from the Angel tube in Islington, this gay café/bar is well worth seeking out. The decor is simple and fresh with a great sense of light and space. The chrome tables are not crowded in on each other and are decorated with fresh flowers. If that doesn't suit, there are plenty of bed sized sofas to relax into. Also newspapers are provided for you to peruse and there's a community notice-board to keep you abreast of all 'the happenings'. All the food is vegetarian and deliciously imaginative. It includes such gems as smoked salmon quiche and polenta and mozarella cheese with grilled vegetables. There's also a 'Guest Meal of the Week' – which is always superb. Pride is taken with the coffee served and the range includes cappuccino, espresso, latte, mocha plus flavoured liqueur coffees. Plus the staff will create if you require – the coffee of your dreams! Give it a try.

CAFE PASTA

8 Theberton Street, N1. 0171 704 9089
Mon to Sat 9.30am-11.30pm   Sun till 11pm
This is an exceptional café with a truly delightful atmosphere. Just off Upper Street, it's ideally placed for Islington's two famous theatres, The Almeida and The King's Head, and only a few minutes stroll from the renowned Camden Passage Antiques Market. The café, on two floors is charming and stylish, with a great dash of originality. On the ground floor the colour scheme is bold and invigorating, set off by imaginative

wall lighting. Fresh flowers are placed on every table and around the room, whilst original paintings and sketches on the walls depict colourful scenes of city life. Upstairs is a revelation: an intimate Edwardian style dining room with views over Theberton and Upper Streets. The atmosphere is warm and inviting, with panelled murals of cascading fruit, ancient urns and vases. A delicate, glittering chandelier and magnificent iron fireplace with a splendid mirror above the mantlepiece add the finishing touches.

The food, delightfully varied and freshly prepared, ranges from French bread sandwiches including melted Swiss cheese, cold roast peppers stuffed with tomatoes in olive oil, to a variety of classic salads and excellent pasta dishes such as fettucine Alfredo. There are always specials of the day and heaven sent pastries and puddings. You're welcome just to linger, read one of the morning papers and sip a superb coffee blended and roasted in Italy, freshly ground for each cup and dispensed via a magnificent red Brasilia machine. High chairs and colouring sheets are provided for children.

In the summer, sit outside under the shade of the canopy, relax and just watch the world go by.

THE RHYTHMIC

89-91 Chapel Market, Islington N1. 0171 713 5859
Mon to Sat 10.30am-2am   Sun 10.30am-Midnight
Britain's Biggest Jazz Venue, fresh, funky and friendly, plays host to music legends from around the world. Here in the evenings you can wine and dine and watch a great show. However during the day Rhythmic dances to a different tune. Layout is divided into two, at the back a glorious Jazz club, at the front a warm, welcoming café bar, with a delightful blues-jazz ambiance. The design is stimulating, with a metal sculpture from Poland suspended from the ceiling, imaginative atmospheric lighting, and the long bar also made of beaten metal. Relax in blue metal chairs from Naples and have your senses stimulated by cool music or indeed from the gentle tinkling of the 'wall of water' fountain from Rome. The owners are passionate about their coffee which is excellent and includes espresso in a tumbler accompanied by mineral water and a chocolate, cappuccino, and cappuccino di lusso, with a variety of natural flavours. If you're feeling decadent, try caffè sfogato, vanilla ice cream in a glass goblet with double espresso poured over. Food is delicious, varied and freshly prepared here including great salads, exquisite Dover sole, club sandwiches, homemade burgers and Spanish omelettes. Excellent puds. After rummaging the antiques and street markets of Islington come here and revive yourself.

CAFE BIANCO

12 Perrins Court NW3. 0171 431 0363

8am-6pm every day or in summer 'till late'

This charming Continental style café is hidden away along a thriving walkway, just off the High Street. The menu is varied, includes vegetarian dishes and changes every day. There are free deliveries locally. The coffee is very good. Because the walkway is traffic free, the café is an ideal place to sit outside with children in a safe environment.

CAFE PASTA

200 Haverstock Hill, Belsize Park, NW3. 0171 431 8531

9.30am -11.30pm every day   Sun till 11pm

After the exhilaration of walking the Heath and drinking up one of London's most spectacular, beloved and historical viewpoints – thousands of years of life stretching away before you into the horizon, – retrace your tracks down the once country roads and stop for a drink of a different sort. Near the top of the hill, in 'the Park Village', is Café Pasta's invitingly airy and relaxed Belsize branch. A drinks bar with delicious flowers, (the smiling staff reflected in the Empire mirror) greets you on arrival. A mass of tables, well spaced with striking sprays of fresh flowers set on colourful tablecloths, allow you to sit discreetly at the back of the room, in the middle of the action, or mannequin-like on display in the front window. (In summer the doors open onto the biggest terrace in London, more than doubling the number of tables.)

The menu here offers the freshest, most imaginative seasonal ingredients cooked to order, with starters and desserts such as tiramisu to make you drool. There is a snack menu served right through the day, though if you're just looking for a quick coup de rouge this is equally possible as the bar is fully licensed throughout the day. The room, covered with wall to wall line drawings of landscapes and landmarks from all over the world, keeps your mind alert, whilst another magnificent gilt mirror reigns serenely over the whole scene as if helping the waiters keep an eye on the tables, explaining the seamless running of the place. This large café seems to be full from morning till night, not least because children are so brilliantly catered for, and so much thought has gone into accessibility for everyone...it isn't in Bel Size for nothing.

CHAMOMILE CAFE

45 England's Lane NW3. 0171 586 4580

7am-6.30pm every day

Two years ago this area of Primrose Hill was a coffee shop desert. Today, thanks to the initiative and ideas of two coffee shop devotees – Suzanne and Nick, it is blessed with a café that seems to effortlessly take into account every taste, need and wish of café and coffee lovers from every walk of life. At any time of day local businessmen, TV celebrities, grandmothers, their children and their grandchildren, students and builders share the happy atmosphere and tuck into the freshly cooked food, or simply revel in a half pint tumbler full of the best café au lait around – clearly worth a visit in itself.

The food is 'healthy' though not at all faddy: a range of all day breakfasts offer free range eggs, lean bacon and organic muesli. Homemade soup at lunchtime is always vegan and there is always one meat and one vegetarian special dish of the day. Fresh salads, omelettes and other dishes use ample amounts of the best ingredients, are beautifully presented and are great value. At midday the trend is very much for take away when the freshly baked, generously filled baguettes are in constant demand. This café could never have become successful without its long list of coffees, each one suiting your mood and never letting you down: dark, aromatic espresso, creamy cappuccino and many others including the trademark tumbler. Accompanied by a selection of freshly baked patisseries and viennoiseries, this café never ceases to offer you exactly what you are looking for.

BREW HOUSE CAFE – KENWOOD HOUSE

Hampstead Lane N6. 0181 341 5384

9am-4 pm every day Summer till 6pm

The Brewhouse was formerly a domestic wing to the famous Kenwood House, home of The Iveagh Bequest, and world famous art treasures. It is set in beautiful parkland and woodland, and adjoins 700 acres of Hampstead Heath. The beautiful lawns run down to a lake, beyond which, on some summer evenings there are concerts when people spread blankets and have picnics as the music floats across the water. So relax here in one of the most beautiful settings in England. You can sit in either the glorious walled gardens, or in what was once the brewhouse and laundry. Then if the mood takes you, stroll around the gardens and terraces of this wonderful country house, or even beyond through the woods to Hampstead Heath. The restaurant features a lunch menu morning bakery and afternoon tea, with a strong sense of English tradition. Coffee is served good and strong and is as popular as ever.

OSHOBASHO CAFE

Highgate Wood, Muswell Hill Road, N10. 0181 444 1505
Tues to Sun 8.30am to half-hour before Park gates close
Open Bank Holidays   Licensed
If you go down to the woods today, you're sure of a big surprise...and a very pleasant one too! For in the heart of this lovely woodland, Basho, the owner, has created an oasis from the ashes of a derelict Cricket Pavilion. Not only is it a great place to sate your appetite – but for many regulars it's a place for spiritual nourishment during the quieter months. To this end, decor is simple and calming with regular painting exhibitions displayed on the wall. The vegetarian cuisine is excellent with a varied and imaginative menu. Food includes yogurt and honey for breakfast, also scrambled eggs, grilled vegetarian sausage with tomatoes and mushrooms. There is a selection of pitta breads, salads, spanish omelette and pastas, and always delicious soup of the day, together with a special. Desserts include an excellent tiramisu. Importantly, the coffee is served with enthusiasm and includes espresso, cappuccino, filtered and decaffeinated. Live music including classical and jazz is often performed in the delightfully spacious gardens, mingling deliciously with the scent of roses and cherry blossom. Not surprisingly, it can become very busy here. So...just relax and enjoy!

THE RAJ ROOM

67 Highgate High Street, N6. 0181 348 8760
8am-11pm every day
A real gem set in the heart of Highgate Village and well worth tracking down. Keep your eyes peeled – it's on the first floor above a high quality clothes shop. D'Arcy, the owner, an Englishman born in India says "I really run this place as a Hill Station somewhere in Darjeeling". It really is a visual and gastronomic delight conveying a riot of colour and textures with books, pictures and ornaments cramming the walls and shelves. Relax – sitting at magnificent farmhouse style tables – and await the pleasures to come: delicious food freshly made on the premises. The menu is enormous and often "Guest Cooks" are to be found producing

their own particular specialities. Regular concoctions include vegan vegetable chilli, through to "Monster" carnivore breakfasts. There is just one kind of coffee available, café au lait, served with great enthusiasm, flare and tradition. The beans are freshly ground for you and then presented in a piping hot jug. Delicious! It is also worth noting that D'Arcy regularly produces "Theme Nights" of poetry, storytelling and music. You can also stay here. There are rooms to suit all tastes and pockets from ambassadors to backpackers.

LA BRIOCHE CAFE
West End Lane, NW6. 0171 431 8175
8.30am-7pm every day
From Holland to the Americas via India, Africa, Asia and Europe, Martin, a cruise personnel manager, finally put his roots down in North London just six months ago. His café is a conglomeration of everything he has found to be good in European cafés. Drawn in by a window display that beats any Dutch master's still life, traditional French wicker bistro chairs invite you to relax at a number of well spaced tables and observe not only the café clientèle but also mirror images of them painted in a witty tableau by Martin's friend Marika. The other walls also grab your attention with action pictures of cooks at work, people and places. Glancing at the menu, Italian bruschetta (mouthwateringly described) are the speciality, with ciabatta, panini, savoury brioches and generously filled baguettes also worth repeat visits for, to be tasted. Breakfasts too are various, ranging from a croissant 'tout simple' to a full cooked breakfast, though the coffee alone is as satisfying – served fresh and strong any way you choose, the traditional Dutch biscuit alongside. One word of advice: do leave room for the most luscious looking homemade cakes you've ever seen. With upbeat music and friendly staff willing to make suggestions if you really are stuck for choice, this is a great place to relax in with the daily papers provided and inwardly digest all that is uplifting in café life today. P.S. Busy at weekends.

FILERIC
12 Queenstown Road, SW8. 0171 720 4844
Mon to Sat 9am-8pm   Sun 9am-5pm
Crossing South of the River to explore – with the impending sense that a currency exchange might have been wise before doing so, fears are instantly dispelled on reaching this destination. The sweetest smell that greets you on arrival may even go so far as to pull tight that knot in your stomach, sending a sudden pang of nostalgia. Such is the startling effect of

finding yourself surrounded by so many gastronomic delights presumed to
be elusively out of reach across an even greater stretch of water – the
Channel. Well, here they all are: 'real' croissants and baguettes prepared in
France, frozen, shipped over here and baked on the spot; Badoit and St
Yorre; le petit Gervais; Rochebaron blue cheese from Beauzac, Epoisses –
in fact over sixty imported cheeses; pâtés; saucisses; fine French wines
including Hydromel, (fermented honey dessert wine of Greek origin, ideal
with foie gras) a '62 Armagnac if you so desire...and...and...the fine
patisseries and savoury tarts are made for the three branches of Fileric, but
you can enjoy them here on the spot in the natural wood 'gallery' at the
back of the shop, where French music and lyrics waft over you as you sip
your fine café au lait and happily reflect on your misgivings about ventu-
ring South of the river which led not only to a treat, but to delights you
could only have found if you really had changed your sterling to francs
and then spent several hours crossing the sea.

CENTREVILLE CAFE JARDIN

41 Tranquil Vale, Blackheath, SE3. 0181 297 9138
Mon to Fri 8.30am-5.30pm   Summer till 9pm
Sat & Sun 8am-6pm   Summer till 9pm
Welcome to France! Well almost. A truly Continental flavour exudes
from this superb café/patisserie. Young, enthusiastic staff and a French
chef ensure you a great experience here. The style is fresh and tasteful,
covering two floors. The ground floor patisserie has bar stools overlooking the street, a comprehensive magazine and newspaper rack, plus a
balcony above the courtyard garden. Below, there are lovely old solid pine
tables, fresh flowers and foliage, and entry to the charming walled
garden. Food is superb, including fresh baked croissants from France and
the popular Gratin du Midi. Also the chef brings about forty French
cheeses over every other week. In the evening excellent pasta dishes are
served. Just sip the good coffee, read a paper, and think about taking
some freshly ground beans home with you. There is free parking in
Blackheath railway station on Saturdays.

ROYAL TEAS

76 Royal Hill, Greenwich, SE10. 0181 691 7240
Mon to Fri 10am-6pm   Sat & Sun 10.30am-6pm
This popular café is a find of such individual charm and character that it
more than merits the stroll up Royal Hill. As soon as you enter you are
enfolded by the warm and cosy atmosphere and the intoxicating aroma
of freshly ground coffee. The environment is intimate and friendly, with

the venue divided into two rooms. The front room is centre of operations as far as coffee is concerned. Here you can get superb cappuccinos
and espressos and also a fine selection of fresh ground coffee beans to
take away. The choice includes pure Costa Rica, Mocha, Colombia and
French roast. Food is all homemade and freshly prepared. Everything is
vegetarian, ranging from super soups to amazing American style breakfasts. Homemade cakes are to die for! It's worth noting that most of the
eating takes place in the back room "parlour" – where children are more
than welcome. Limited table seating is available outside fronting the
premises.

THE TEA HOUSE
14 King William Walk, Greenwich, SE10. 0181 858 0803
Mon to Sun 10am-6pm (later in summer)
Situated literally just yards away from the glorious Greenwich Park, this
is superbly located for such gems as the Old Royal Observatory and the
Cutty Sark. A lovely building, dating back to the 18th Century and still
retaining the original wall panelling, it has been updated, creating a
spacious, clean and fresh environment with sturdy pine chairs and tables,
and wooden floors. During the summer you can sit in the secluded garden and enjoy the dappled shade of cherry and magnolia trees or out in
front watching Greenwich life pass by. All coffee is excellent and served
generously from cafetières. It includes varieties such as Kenyan and
Colombian. Flavoured coffees, changed daily, include Dutch, Vanilla or
Grand Marnier. Food is simple and good, including superb freshly made
sandwiches and sumptuous cakes ideal for a picnic in the park. The friendly staff will also put together a hamper for you, given enough notice.

PISTACHIOS CAFE
15 Nelson Road, Greenwich, SE10.   0181 853 0602
Monday to Sunday 9am-6pm
A glorious venue in the heart of Greenwich Village, on a bustling street
of bookshops, antiques, galleries, restaurants, and other attractions. Here
you are assured a warm welcome in a stress free environment where you
can just sip good coffee, meet friends, or dive into the enormous menu.
The café is stylish with bold colours contrasting with wooden floorboards
and soothing wall lighting.There's plenty of space and flowers on the
tables. At the back is the room known as the marquee, a terrific space,
perfect for summer, looking onto the landscaped garden where you can
also sit and relax in seclusion, overlooked only by the magnificent
St. Alfege church. Choice of food here is vast and made on the premises

using the freshest possible ingredients. Specials include superb vegetarian soups, Italian pasta bake, and salads. There are amazing sandwiches bagels and baguettes with fillings that include hot brie and cranberry, banana and maple syrup, and smoked salmon. The owners are enthusiastic about coffee and have devised their own blend of choice arabica beans.

REVIVAL CAFE AND HALES GALLERY

70 Deptford High Street, SE8. 0181 694 1194

Mon to Sat 9am-5pm

Revival's great location has a vibrancy and colour that can really only come from a multi-cultural environment, especially evident on market days. The café has a roomy, light atmosphere with tasteful and imaginative decor. Refreshingly, there's plenty of room between the tables. So sit back and relax, take a newspaper provided or admire the works of art adorning the walls. Outside there is a peaceful courtyard garden, adding further to the convivial atmosphere. It's certainly worth noting that there is a Gallery (Hales) of some repute located in the basement, tending to specialise in sculptures and the occasional installation. Food here really is excellent, leaning towards vegetarian, but not exclusively. It's all made fresh on the premises daily and includes wonderful homemade wholemeal bread and scones. Other dishes are cheese and almond broccoli bake, smoked salmon and dill quiche, pasta, soups, chicken salad and a variety of superb sandwiches on different breads. The owners are terribly enthusiastic about the Lavazza coffee they serve. It includes espresso, cappuccino, decaffeinated, au lait and latte, served by always genial staff.

HOME BREWING METHODS

by Mary Banks

The rules for coffee brewing

1 Use fresh, cold water. (Not chemically softened.)
2 Use water just off the boil. (92-96 C degrees)
3 Be generous with coffee.(55-60 grams per litre of water.)
4 Serve and drink as soon as possible after brewing.
5 Keep all equipment spotlessly clean.
6 Never reheat coffee or keep it hot more than 45 minutes.

Hygiene

Coffee has a high oil content and residue on equipment can quickly become rancid. Equipment and storage containers should therefore be kept spotlessly clean. Brewing equipment should be descaled regularly. All equipment should be rinsed thoroughly after washing in a mild cleanser (vinegar and bicarbonate of soda are excellent).

Key to Measures

I tablespoon = 5.7 grams of coffee
I heaped teaspoon = 2.5 grams of coffee
$4^{1}/_{2}$-5 tablespoons per pint = 55-60 grams per litre.
(spoon sizes are imperial measures)

The Ibrik

Grind of Coffee used: pulverised – very fine
Recommended Measure: One heaped teaspoon to one demi-tasse of water per serving. If a sweet brew is required one level teaspoon of sugar should be added to the brew for each serving.

The Jug

Grind of Coffee used: coarse
Recommended Measure: 55-60 grams of coffee per litre of water. $4^{1}/_{2}$-5 tablespoons to one pint. Leave to stand for 4 minutes before serving.

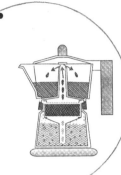

Domestic Espresso Pot
Grind of coffee used: very fine
Degree of roast used: dark
Recommended Measure: coffee should fill the basket, not loosely, but rather compactly

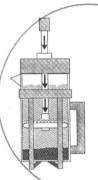

Plunger Pot
Grind of Coffee used: Medium
Recommended Measure: 55-60 grams of coffee per litre of water. $4^{1}/_{2}$ -5 tablespoons to one pint. Leave to stand for 3-4 minutes before plunging.

Electric Filter Machine
Grind of Coffee used: Fine
Recommended Measure: 55-60 grams of coffee per litre of water. $4^{1}/_{2}$ - 5 tablespoons to one pint.

Vacuum or Glass balloon
Grind of Coffee used: Medium to fine
Recommended Measure: 55-60 grams of coffee per litre of water. $4^{1}/_{2}$ - 5 tablespoons to one pint.

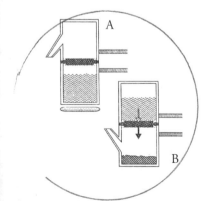

Neapolitan
Grind of Coffee used: medium
Recommended Measure: 55-60 grams of coffee per litre of water. $4^{1}/_{2}$ - 5 tablespoons to one pint. When the water has boiled and steam exits from the side vent the machine is inverted (b).

INDEX